START AND RUN A PROFITABLE RETAIL BUSINESS
A step-by-step business plan

Michael M. Coltman, M.B.A.

Self-Counsel Press
(a division of)
International Self-Counsel Press Ltd.
Canada U.S.A.

Printed in Canada

First edition: October, 1983; April, 1987
Second edition: January, 1989; Reprinted: September, 1990
Third edition: November, 1993

Canadian Cataloguing in Publication Data

Coltman, Michael M. (Michael MacDonald), 1930
   Start and run a profitable retail business

(Self-counsel business series)
ISBN 0-88908-767-9

1. Retail trade —Canada— Management. 2. Stores, Retail—Canada—
Management. I. Title. II. Series.
HF5429.6.C2C66 1993   658.8'701'0971   C93-091807-X

Cover photography by Terry Guscott, ATN Visuals, Vancouver, B.C.

Self-Counsel Press
(*a division of*)
International Self-Counsel Press Ltd.

1481 Charlotte Road
North Vancouver, British Columbia
V7J 1H1

1704 N. State Street
Bellingham, Washington
98225

CONTENTS

SAMPLES

1
INTRODUCTION

Retailers have successfully existed in North America since the early trappers traded with the larger companies (the monopolists of their day) who were in business at that time. Not much has changed. Today large companies still tend to monopolize many markets, but small business retailers nevertheless continue to thrive and grow by filling a niche that the larger companies are not geared to fill.

Most large companies depend on small business retailers. For example, large companies mass produce manufactured goods. Other large companies distribute, transport, and wholesale those goods. But they all depend on retailers to sell them to the ultimate consumer — and most of these retailers are small business operators.

a. RISK INVOLVED

If you are entering the retail business field for the first time, you need to know about the risks involved. Those who go into small business do so in spite of, or in ignorance of, the odds of survival. A rule of thumb for new small businesses is that as many as 50% fail during the first year, and as many as 90% in less than five years.

Analysis of business failures shows that as many as 95% of these failures are caused by lack of competence and managerial experience in that particular business. This lack of competence shows up in such things as:

(a) Poor planning

(b) An inadequate market analysis

(c) Product defects

(d) Lack of proper marketing and/or advertising

(e) Poor start-up timing

(f) Failure to anticipate the competition

(g) Unanticipated costs

(h) Continual shortage of working capital

(i) Failure to keep proper financial records

(j) Unexpected business problems for which the owner is not trained or prepared to cope

(k) Failure to stay familiar with trends in the type of business the owner is in

(l) Inadequate inventory control, such as failing to mark down overstocked inventory in order to move it

(m) Poor control of credit extended to customers

b. HARD WORK

Suppose you read the following in the help wanted section of your local newspaper:

> Worker wanted for new retail business. Must like hard work and interaction with public. No previous experience necessary. Responsible for business 24 hours a day, 7 days a week. Duties, in addition to overall management, include purchasing, receiving, inventory control, bookkeeping, hiring, personnel, payroll, maintenance and janitorial, government relations, advertising and public relations,

credit, sales, customer complaints. No vacation for first 3 years. Salary will depend on profits. Some risk of losing personal possessions such as car, furnishings, personal residence, and spouse and family, leading to permanent nervous condition.

If this ad were run by a large company, you probably wouldn't even bother applying, but the conditions outlined above are typical of the small retail business.

However, this hypothetical ad is misleading since it seems to imply that because you have total responsibility you are the "boss." That is only partly true. Many people (suppliers, employees, customers) are going to make demands on your time and, in many respects, they are your "bosses."

In other words, don't fool yourself if your reason for going into business is because you're tired of working for, and taking orders from, someone else. You can become just as bored and frustrated working for yourself as you can for anyone else and, in addition, you'll be working a lot harder, for longer hours, and possibly initially for less money. And you'll still be taking orders from your customers!

Running your own business does not mean that you'll be able to do exactly what you please when you want to do it. In fact you could end up doing what others associated with your business have failed to do, and at times that aren't very convenient to you.

Therefore, to be satisfied in your own mind that you still want to start your own retail business, find out in advance everything you can about the particular type of retail business you want to begin.

Refer to books and periodicals that will give you background information. Contact your local colleges and/or universities since they often teach courses and have reference material relating to small businesses.

Talk to owners and employees. If possible, work (without pay if necessary) in a retail store of the kind you think you would enjoy running.

c. CHARACTERISTICS FOR SUCCESS

Numerous studies have been conducted to determine the characteristics that make a successful small business entrepreneur. There is no general consensus about what constitutes the right blend of characteristics, since what is important in one individual may be less important in another. Also, the type of products or services that you are dealing with can have a bearing.

In general, the following characteristics, to a greater or lesser extent, and in some combination, appear to be important:

(a) Drive or energy and the willingness to take responsibility, take risks, make decisions, and accept the consequences

(b) Personal initiative and the ability to not rely on others to get the ball rolling or defer decisions to others or to committees

(c) Personality and human relations ability. This includes matters such as emotional stability, sociability, cheerfulness in adversity, cooperation, tact, and consideration for others.

(d) Organizational ability with an eye to detail so that those around you don't have to guess about what needs to be done and who has to do it

(e) Written and oral communication skills. You have to be able to communicate with employees, suppliers, customers, bankers, and all the other people you have to deal with daily.

(f) Administrative ability in planning, setting goals and objectives, deciding how to measure results, controlling the business, interpreting financial statements, and similar matters

(g) Technical knowledge about the business. This means not only knowing what you do know but also where you may be deficient in certain skills and technical abilities so that you can upgrade yourself or hire employees competent in that area.

(h) Good judgment, patience, and restraint

(i) Leadership

Looking over that list you might think that nobody could ever survive in the business world. However, this is only a list of desirable characteristics that are helpful in most situations. Lacking one or several of them will not necessarily lead to failure.

1. Willingness to work hard

However, there is one characteristic that is absolutely essential, and that is the willingness to work hard. Without that, in a small business, you are almost certainly doomed to failure since you have the sole responsibility for the ultimate success or failure of your business.

If you do work hard you should achieve success. That success is measured not only in having a profitable business, but also in the rewards that are less easy to measure, such as being satisfied with your working environment, being your own boss, having pride in company ownership, enjoying status in the community, and owning an outlet for creative ideas.

Before you embark on a business venture of your own it might be a good idea to try the self-test in Worksheet #1. After each question check the answer that comes closest to how you rate yourself. It is important to be honest with yourself. Do the test now.

Now count up your score:

(a) Number of check marks in the left column:_____

(b) Number of check marks in the center column:_____

(c) Number of check marks in the right column:_____

If most of your check marks are in the left column, you probably have the right qualities to run your own business. If not, your chances of success are considerably lower and it might be a good idea to work with a partner who is stronger in the areas where you have a weakness.

If most of your checks are in the right column, not even a great partner will be able to prop you up.

On the other hand, a good score in the above test is no guarantee of success — all the other elements of a successful business must be in place to ensure that.

The test was primarily designed to give you an insight into your relative strengths and weaknesses. If you have any weaknesses, you should decide how you are going to overcome them.

2. Other questions

In addition to the above questions, you should also honestly answer the following:

(a) Do I have the mental and physical stamina to run my own business?

(b) Am I prepared to sacrifice my present lifestyle to this new venture?

(c) Are my spouse and family (if any) willing to accept the change and possible upheaval in lifestyle?

(d) How much income do I need to survive during this period of change? Can I survive if all my income has to come from a new venture that may or may not be successful?

If the answer to each of these questions is not a definite yes, then it is possible you may be acting on emotion rather than in an objective way. In that case, if you do not succeed, you have only yourself to blame.

SELF-TEST

Good Average Poor

1. I have the determination to finish what I set out to do.
2. I work well with others.
3. I have the respect and confidence of those whom I supervise.
4. I get along well with people in general.
5. I am a good organizer.
6. I communicate well with others.
7. I am able to motivate others to work well.
8. I know my limitations and don't try to go beyond them.
9. I listen well.
10. I am able to take valuable advice.
11. I can handle pressure calmly.
12. I enjoy competition.
13. I have imagination and creativity.
14. I am good at solving problems.
15. I can handle detail and tie up loose ends.

d. RETIREMENT AND RUNNING YOUR OWN BUSINESS

If you are retired, or close to it, you may be planning to start your own small retail business. If that is the case, your objective is probably to have a relatively trouble-free business that provides you with a secure income and permits you to plan for its disposition in your estate.

Be cautious. It may not be easy to start a business that is profitable in the short run, and if you have to use pension funds or cash from an insurance policy to start a business, you may be taking a great risk.

Also, if you have been an employee of a larger business throughout your career,

you will find the risks and strains of running your own business quite different, and perhaps even impossible to adapt to after 40 or more years of working for an organization where you merely followed policies and procedures decided by others.

You may find yourself working six days a week in a retail store, or even seven days a week if you buy a restaurant. Holidays may never materialize unless you can afford to pay for a manager in your absence.

If the business you plan to start is quite different from the one you have previously worked in you may suddenly find you don't like it. One way to decide this is to take a job, part-time if necessary, in that

4

kind of business to help confirm it is what you want before you risk your hard-earned savings or pension funds.

Finally, in your own retail business the decisions you make will be all yours. There may be no one to turn to for help, or to blame if things go wrong.

e. ADVANTAGES AND DISADVANTAGES OF STARTING A NEW BUSINESS

There are both advantages and disadvantages to starting a new business and you should be aware of these in order to consider the alternative of purchasing an already existing retail business.

1. Advantages

Some of the advantages of starting a new business are as follows:

(a) You can select a location that takes advantage of current economic or market conditions.

(b) If the plans include constructing a new building, the building can be designed to your specifications and the type of business you plan to have. A new building can be designed to meet conditions as they exist today.

(c) There may be an appeal to potential customers about a new business being opened. Curiosity alone may help you attract a good starting clientele.

(d) You can stock an inventory for today's trends. This can be particularly useful if you have an exclusive on new products.

2. Disadvantages

Some of the disadvantages of starting a new business are as follows:

(a) If land and building are involved, the time required to put together a building package and financing to buy the necessary land can be quite long and the financing itself fairly complex.

(b) A clientele will have to be built up. This takes time — anywhere from a few months in some businesses to two to three years in others. Starting a new business does not, by itself, create an immediate clientele or market.

(c) Building up a clientele also delays a return on your own investment and during this time interest will have to be paid on any borrowed money.

(d) A new business, designed and located based on future demand for its products and/or services may require you to keep advancing the company new cash to keep it in operation.

(e) Any new business suffers an additional risk since it will probably have to compete with already existing businesses whose sites and/or locations are more favorable and whose business is already successfully established.

If you feel that the above disadvantages outweigh the advantages, you should then seriously consider the alternative of purchasing an already successful retail business.

Another alternative might be to try to reduce the risk by starting a new business on a franchised basis. Franchising is discussed in a later chapter.

2
TYPES OF RETAIL BUSINESSES

Once you are sure you wish to start your own new retail business, the first step is to decide on the type of retail business you would like.

a. TYPES OF BUSINESSES

Retail businesses can be classified into two types: those that handle products of various kinds, commonly referred to as retailers, and those that offer services, commonly referred to as service businesses. Obviously, some businesses operate as both retail and service companies that handle products and provide services.

1. Retailers

There are two basic kinds of retailers: there are those who work on a personal basis with their customers, often with an office in the home. This is often called direct sales. The others work from a store or shop location.

Both types of retailers must seek and attract customers. For this reason, sales may be very dependent on advertising. Some of the more common retailing businesses include:

Appliances

Auto parts and supplies

Bakeries

Book and stationery stores

Building materials

Clothing

Department stores

Drug stores

Dry goods and general merchandise

Electronic appliances

Flowers and/or potted plants

Fuel dealer

Furniture

Garden equipment and supplies

Gas stations

General merchandise

Gifts and novelties

Groceries

Hardware

Heating and air conditioning

Home furnishings

Jewelry, watches, diamonds

Mail order houses

Medical, surgical, hospital supplies

Mobile homes

New and used cars

Office equipment and supplies

Photographic equipment and supplies

Plumbing and heating

Radios, TVs, music

Restaurants

Roofing and siding

Shoes

Sporting goods

Tobacconist

Toys and hobbies

Variety goods

Vending machines

2. Service firms

Generally, service firms are categorized as those that are not directly involved in offering a tangible product that is bought and sold. Although there may be products or parts involved, it is primarily the work skill or the service of the business's employees that the customer is paying for. Some of the more common service businesses include:

Accounting

Advertising agency

Athletic clubs

Auto parking

Auto and auto body repair

Bowling alleys

Car rental and leasing

Communications

Consulting and public relations

Coin operated laundries

Computer and data processing services

Dance schools

Dental laboratories

Drive-in theaters

Drycleaning/laundry

Duplicating service

Engineering/scientific service

Equipment rental and leasing

Funeral services

Hotels and motels

Insurance

Legal firms

Movie theaters

Outdoor advertising

Photo studios

Radio and TV repair

Real estate

Travel agency

b. PRODUCT TYPES

Retail, or consumer, products present their own particular characteristics that require different merchandising skills depending on the type of product. Retail products can generally be classified as convenience products, shopping products, or specialty products.

1. Convenience products

Convenience products are items that the consumer wishes to buy with the minimum of effort and whose price is not an important consideration. Convenience food stores are typical of an outlet for convenience products. They offer staple items of relatively low value that customers want as quickly as possible and that they may not be able to buy anywhere else at the time the items are needed.

Merchandising convenience products generally does not require highly qualified sales personnel. Proximity to competitors is not a problem since such stores often are open when others are closed.

The variety of product lines they carry is also limited to the most likely items that customers will want in an emergency. The layout of convenience stores is important since the profit realized from sale of impulse items can be considerable.

2. Shopping products

Shopping products are those for which purchasers shop around before buying to compare prices, quality, fashion, level of service, and similar factors. Shopping goods are not purchased as frequently as convenience products since their prices are relatively higher.

Most household goods, clothing, and cars are examples of products for which the customer generally spends a considerable time making comparisons before deciding to purchase.

For these types of products, fairly knowledgeable sales personnel are required and they should be paid accordingly since their ability to explain the advantages of your products over competitive lines is important and their ability to influence customers in determining value for money is essential.

Surprisingly, retail stores selling shopping products of similar types are often found close to each other since this provides the customers a convenient method of shopping around and making comparisons.

3. Specialty products

Specialty products are invariably of relatively high value, but this high value is not a major concern to prospective purchasers who are more concerned with quality, or at least perceived quality. Examples are jewelry and high class clothing. Purchasers will not be deterred by having to seek out a shop that carries the product brand they want.

Attractiveness of the store and high levels of service are sometimes more important than for convenience or shopping products. Discount price sales are not a major consideration but advertising can be more widespread since prospective purchasers will travel farther to buy the brand they desire.

Not all retail products fall neatly into one of the three broad categories outlined. There is a lot of overlap of products, and even of customers. What one customer considers a convenience item another might consider a shopping product. What is important to you, as a potential product retailer, is knowing your market and how its customers perceive your products.

c. CHARACTERISTICS FOR PRODUCT SURVIVAL

Regardless of the business you eventually choose to start, there are some general characteristics that seem to determine which products survive in the marketplace. These characteristics suggest that a product will survive if it —

(a) has a relatively large market and there is no dominant supplier (that is, it is not a monopolistic situation),

(b) is similar to other products that have survived and is as acceptable as those other products,

(c) is easily recognizable,

(d) has one or more advantages (such as appearance, packaging, price, or performance) over its competitors, and

(e) can be upgraded to keep it competitive if the need arises, or abandoned when its life cycle is over.

1. Specific questions

When deciding on products to carry, consider the following questions:

(a) Is it a high priced item that customers might hesitate to buy?

(b) Alternatively, is it such a low priced item that it will only provide an overall reasonable profit if it is sold in volume and, if so, can you buy it in bulk?

(c) Where is the product source and will the product be available on an uninterrupted basis?

(d) Who provides the product warranty if one is required?

(e) Who provides and pays for repair service if it is required?

(f) Is the product complex and difficult to use?

(g) If product assembly is required, do you need to do this before selling it?

(h) If the product is heavy/bulky, will you provide a delivery service?

(i) Is the product seasonal? If so, what alternative products can you sell in the "off" season?

(j) Is the product only a fad, gimmick, or novelty item that isn't worth stocking on a long-term basis?

Be rational in product selection. Don't let personal bias mislead you. You might like purple painted plastic ceiling mobiles, but your potential customers may not share your preference.

d. WHICH PARTICULAR BUSINESS?

Given the wide variety of types of businesses and products there are to choose from, which one should you, as an entrepreneur, select?

Obviously, you should select a growth business in preference to any other. How do you find out which are the growth businesses? That's a more difficult question to answer since a growth business this year may be a declining business next year due to changing technology, or changing consumer demands. For example, mechanical calculators were a growth business until electronic calculators came along.

1. Helpful organizations

The following organizations, among others, can frequently offer valuable information and advice concerning expected growth rates in various industries:

(a) Banks (particularly if they have business development departments separate from their normal banking activities)

(b) The Federal Business Development Bank (Canada)

(c) The Federal Department of Industry, Trade and Commerce (Canada)

(d) The Small Business Administration (U.S.)

(e) Venture capital companies (more about these in a later chapter on financing)

The above organizations can also be very helpful to you in other ways, as can government departments involved in small business development.

You should also consult your local trade associations and/or Chambers of Commerce, and libraries (both general and university/college libraries), particularly if they have business sections.

2. Compatibility with goals

It is also important to be aware of the working hours and requirements of any business that you are contemplating starting. You need to seek out a business that is compatible with your ideals and goals, as well as your lifestyle.

For example, if you do not like working 12 or more hours a day, 7 days a week, then you should probably stay away from the restaurant business.

You must also decide if you want to run the business directly yourself or buy one that is large enough for "absentee" ownership where you can hire a manager to run it.

3. Funding required

Finally, you must, even at this early stage, have some idea of the amount of money you have available or wish to invest. Financing will be covered in some depth in later chapters, but if you have only, let us say, $5,000 cash that you can put into a business, it might be unwise to raise your sights too high by investigating a business that requires a total investment of $100,000.

Regardless of outside cash that you may be able to raise, it is a general rule of thumb that you will have to put up at least 10% of the required cash yourself, and even as much as 25%. Therefore, if you only have $5,000 cash you should be looking for a business whose total start-up cost is in the $20,000 to $50,000 range.

e. SEEKING OPPORTUNITIES

In order to start up a new retail business, you must seek out information about the type of business and profit opportunities that meet your ambitions and cash availability. Some ways to do this are:

(a) Newspaper classified advertisements, particularly those in the business opportunities section

(b) Trade journals specializing in advertising businesses of the type you are looking for

(c) Word-of-mouth from contacts you have in the type of business you are contemplating starting

(d) Your local Chamber of Commerce or Board of Trade is familiar with many businesses in the local area

(e) Trade sources of the type of business you are looking for can be an excellent information bank. These trade sources include the suppliers, manufacturers, distributors, and trade associations.

(f) Accountants, business consultants, and lawyers all work with small business owners and are often aware of profitable businesses to start and how much investment is required. If you don't have an accountant or a lawyer already, you are going to need their services. In your selection of these professionals you can sound them out about their awareness of retail business opportunities.

(g) Your local bank manager may be able to help. Businesses need financing. Much of this may be bank financing. Your own bank manager, through information from other branches, may be aware of profitable businesses that the bank has financed.

You should also be familiar with the types of businesses that are not very profitable at the time you are looking.

One way to do this is to search out information on bankruptcies and see if they are happening in large numbers in the type of business that you are contemplating starting.

Credit granting companies such as Dun and Bradstreet are a good source for this type of information. For example, Dun and Bradstreet produces a business failure record by type of retail business on an annual basis. They also produce an annual publication entitled Key Business Ratios that provides some key financial data about various types of retail and service businesses.

You might contact the closest office of that company to obtain the most recent annual statistics, which may be useful in helping you decide on the type of business to be in. The statistical information provided in the pamphlet will also be useful later on, as you will see in the chapters on market and financial planning.

3
PROFESSIONAL HELP

In starting up your new retail business you are going to need some professional help from a banker, accountant, lawyer, and possibly other specialists and consultants.

a. BANKER

For most small businesses a small local bank branch is likely to be of more help than a big city bank that handles only large accounts. You should advise your banker of your intention to start a business and keep him or her informed of your progress.

Consider your bank not just as a place to store money, but also as a possible provider of the following services:

  (a) Credit references on your customers or potential customers

  (b) Financial and investment advice

  (c) Money to start and eventually to expand your business

  (d) Check certification

  (e) Safety deposit box

  (f) Night depository

  (g) Payroll and other accounting services

Wherever possible, try to find a bank that is close to your business, at least for daily deposit of receipts since this will minimize the risk of losing them on the way to the bank.

Your banker will probably be able to provide you with useful information about the type of retail business you plan to start. For example, your banker probably handles the accounts of retail businesses similar to the type you are planning to start and

can help you evaluate your financial forecasts (discussed in more detail later).

Once you are in business, it is important to keep your banker informed of the business's progress. Your banker is interested in having you succeed since you, as a customer of the bank, are a potential source of profit to the bank.

b. ACCOUNTANT

If you do not have qualifications in accounting, you will need an accountant to at least handle your annual tax return. Tax law and tax accounting for businesses can be quite complex. Few small business owners have the competence or the time to be knowledgeable about all of the intricacies of income tax.

This does not mean that you should not try to familiarize yourself with income tax rules and regulations, since that knowledge can be helpful in the day-to-day operation of any business, but a professional advisor in this area is well worth the cost.

An accountant can also help you set up your initial accounting and control system, including design of forms, and help you select your equipment such as an office calculator, sales register, or even a computer and software.

As well as preparing your periodic financial statements, an accountant can interpret and analyze them for you and advise on growth possibilities for your company when it is well established.

Once your accountant and banker have been selected, they should meet. In areas such as financing and tax planning, the two of them will need to consult.

c. LAWYER

Finally, you will probably need a lawyer since there are always some legal matters to be taken care of in starting a business. One is the legal form of your organization (this is discussed in chapter 4).

Other matters where legal advice is useful for a person starting and operating a small retail business might include the rights of:

(a) Buyers and sellers of merchandise

(b) Landlords and tenants

(c) Creditors and debtors

(d) Employers and employees

(e) Purchasers and sellers of land and/or buildings

(f) Borrowers and lenders of money

A lawyer can also check such items as licensing requirements and rental contracts, as well as make you aware of any special governmental requirements that may exist for your type of business.

Use a lawyer who will tell you in advance the cost of his or her service — even the cost of an initial meeting.

Once you select your lawyer and accountant, it might be a good idea to have them get together since some of their areas of concern can also overlap and you do not want to pay twice for the same advice or time.

d. CONSULTANTS

One type of consultant that you will probably need is an insurance agent, since some forms of insurance will have to be arranged before you start business (see chapter 22).

Although it is doubtful that you will need other consultants to start your business, you may need some special managerial or marketing consultants as your business expands.

Specialists can advise in areas such as business layout, inventory control, business organization, advertising campaigns, and many similar areas where you need special help at a particular time.

These specialists, since they are not involved in day-to-day operations as you will be, can often view your business in a more objective way and give professional advice to help you improve your profits.

Consulting services have expertise in preparing feasibility studies for new business proposals, searching out good sites, documenting loan proposals, and similar services. Their fees can run from reasonable to unreasonable.

A word of caution about consultants: There are many who charge more than their advice is worth. Since there are no licensing, certification, or competency requirements for consultants, anyone (even another retailer between stores) can promote himself or herself as a consultant with the sole intention of extracting money from you.

In particular, be wary of consultants who offer to find you money for a fee based on the amount of money raised — for example, 10% of the $200,000 that you need, or $20,000. A reputable lender would probably not lend money if an intermediary were involved for such an exorbitant fee.

e. CHOOSING YOUR PROFESSIONAL ADVISORS

To select professional advisors, you should shop around. Bankers, accountants, and lawyers, like all business people, are in competition with each other.

Also, even though these professionals (particularly accountants and lawyers) are members of professional associations and must demonstrate competence in their field, there are degrees of competency, and of specialization. Do not choose the first one you visit because of a positive impression, even though that first impression can be important in your final decision.

Let each professional know that you are discussing the situation with two or three others in that profession. This way, they may not charge you for a short initial meeting since this may encourage you to stay with them in the long run.

Check with friends who are in business, or even with people you meet socially or on other business matters, about professionals they could recommend.

However, do not choose a professional advisor solely because you know him or her socially. Try to find a lawyer or accountant who is familiar with the type of retail business you propose to start.

If you plan to locate in a particular area, selecting a lawyer, an accountant, and a banker in that area can be preferable since they will be familiar with local conditions and will be easier to visit when necessary.

1. Be prepared for questions

Professional advisors are going to ask you questions almost from the outset. You should try to have the answers to these questions ready, even in an exploratory first meeting.

These questions (many of which will be discussed in detail in later chapters) will include such matters as the type and size of business you are thinking of starting, the organizational form of your company (proprietorship, partnership, or private limited company), how much money you can invest yourself, how much money you may have to borrow, and when you plan to start the business.

2. Cost of professionals

You will want to know how much you are going to pay for professional advice. Bankers do not normally charge for their time. Their profit is made from the interest rate they charge you for money that you borrow from them and for the use they can make of business funds you have on deposit in accounts with them.

Accountants and lawyers usually charge on an hourly basis, or alternatively charge an annual retainer fee for certain ongoing day-to-day advice, with an extra charge for matters that fall outside what is included in the retainer. In order to minimize your costs, a retainer approach is probably not a good idea unless your business is going to require a great deal of professional advice.

If your accountant is also going to produce your monthly accounts, there will likely be a flat monthly charge for doing this. Filing the annual tax return might be included in this monthly charge. Alternatively, that may be an additional annual cost.

Since accountants and lawyers do have a fairly high hourly fee, try to minimize the amount of time you use them. As much as possible, make decisions for yourself and only call on them when a matter to be resolved is critical and where proper professional help is required.

Also, check at the outset what the procedure is for advice. Generally, accountants and lawyers, like most business people, prefer to arrange face to face meetings with as much advance notice as possible. Finally, they generally prefer not to give advice over the telephone concerning important matters that require documentation.

f. BUSINESS REGULATIONS

A word at this point about business regulations: depending on the type of retail business you plan to open you must be familiar with, and conform to, any necessary business regulations.

Regulations can cover such matters as permits, licenses, zoning, land use, taxes of various kinds, building codes, business registration, organizational form, labor regulations, and many more.

These regulations depend on a number of factors about your business (such as its type and geographic location) and for that reason you should determine which regulations are relevant in your particular case.

Your business advisors, and in particular your lawyer and accountant, can be very helpful in this regard. But even your insurance agent or consultant could advise you on such things as fire codes.

4
LEGAL FORMS OF BUSINESS ORGANIZATION

Once you have decided to open a particular type of business, and you are sure you have the right qualities to succeed, one of the earliest decisions that you have to make is the legal organizational form that the enterprise will take. The three common types of organization are the proprietorship, the partnership, and the limited company.

a. PROPRIETORSHIP

The easiest way for you to establish an organization with little or no cost or legal problems is to operate as a proprietorship. Many retail businesses are operated this way, with the owner responsible for the actions and liabilities of the business, even if the day-to-day running of it, or parts of it, is delegated to others.

As a proprietorship you are financed primarily from your personal savings, from bank loans, sometimes from government loans, and, if the business is successful, from the profits of the business reinvested in it.

The profit of the proprietorship is the personal income of the owner and is taxed, with any salary paid to him or her by the business, at personal tax rates. Any loans from creditors or investors are made to the owner and not to the company.

Proprietorships do not issue shares of any kind, as do limited companies (to be discussed later). Businesses established as proprietorships must still conform to regulatory authorities, such as local licensing authorities, in order to obtain a license to legally operate as a business.

1. Advantages

The main advantages of a proprietorship are that as owner you have total control, do not have to consider the opinions of partners or other business associates (thus speeding the decision-making process), and will reap the full financial rewards for your efforts.

There are also minimal legal restrictions with a proprietorship and it can be easily discontinued if and when this might be appropriate.

2. Disadvantages

Some disadvantages are that, theoretically, the organization ceases to exist when the owner dies and the assets of the company become part of the owner's estate and are subject to estate and inheritance taxes. Thus it may be difficult for relatives to continue the business.

A proprietorship may also find it difficult to expand since it does not have the same opportunities to raise capital as do other types of business organizations that have a broader base of financial resources.

Also, generally speaking, in case of bankruptcy or a serious lawsuit you may find that your personal assets (such as your house, car, and personal savings) as well as the company's assets may be seized to satisfy the liabilities of the organization. In other words, the proprietorship's liability is unlimited. This is probably the major disadvantage of a proprietorship.

b. PARTNERSHIP

Unlike the sole proprietorship, the partnership is generally a more formal type of business organization. It is a legal association between two or more individuals as co-owners of a business.

Although a partnership does not require a written agreement, all partners probably should agree to a negotiated contract, or articles of partnership. The terms of these articles vary widely from one enterprise to another, but they should include at least the name of the company; the name of each partner; the rights, contributions, and benefits of each partner; how the profits and losses are to be distributed (without an agreement to the contrary they are assumed to be distributed equally); and the length of the life of the partnership.

In a partnership, each partner may represent the company and enter into contracts on its behalf. Each partner is also personally liable for the debts of the company incurred by other partners. This personal liability (as with a proprietorship) is unlimited.

Partnerships are not taxed at the limited company tax rates. Instead, the business's net income, or loss, is shared according to the terms of the partnership contract, and each partner includes that share, plus any salary received from the company, on his or her personal tax return.

Partnerships, like proprietorships, do not issue shares of any kind and must conform to regulatory authorities.

1. Advantages

The main advantages of partnerships are that they are relatively easy to organize, financing is sometimes easier to obtain, and (since there is more than one owner) the total partnership investment can be much greater than in a proprietorship. A partnership may also have a greater depth of combined judgment and managerial skills.

2. Disadvantages

Disadvantages are that, except in the case of limited partnerships (discussed later), upon one partner's death or withdrawal from the business, the partnership may have to be dissolved and reorganized. This can make it difficult to continue the company's operations.

It can also create financial difficulties for the business if the dead partner's heirs disagree with the company's evaluation of his or her share of the company. Also, the heirs have to be bought out, which may impose a financial burden on the remaining partners.

Another disadvantage of the partnership is that, since in many cases all partners may need to be consulted, quick decisions about the company's operations may be difficult to make and serious disagreements can occur.

Also, partners are not only responsible for the debts and obligations they have contracted for, but they are also responsible for those contracted by all other partners.

Finally, it may be difficult to remove an incompetent partner or one you don't get along with. Difficulties often arise with partners concerning the direction the business should take and how it should be run. Sometimes considerable interpersonal skills are necessary to overcome these difficulties.

However, these difficulties in themselves can also be opportunities since, in discussing them, mutually agreeable objectives and plans often materialize. This, in itself, can be an advantage compared to operating as a proprietorship where you may have no one knowledgeable about your business to discuss it with.

To minimize areas of conflict in a partnership you might consider including in the partnership agreement details concerning the following typical questions:

(a) Who is responsible for various aspects of the business, for example, production and marketing?

(b) Who establishes operating policies and, indeed, what constitutes a policy? Are policies, or changes of policies, decided by a majority vote of the partners, or by some other method?

(c) What expenses (for example, car mileage or entertainment expenses) can be charged to the business?

3. Limited partnership

Up to this point, the partnership type of organization discussed is what is referred to as a general partnership. There is another form of partnership known as limited partnership.

A limited partnership has both general partners with unlimited personal liability, and limited partners with limited personal liability. The partnership contract should spell out this limited personal liability. It should also indicate the amount that the limited partner(s) have invested.

A limited partnership arrangement is made when limited, or silent, partners wish to invest in a company and obtain a return on their investment without being personally involved in the day-to-day decision making and operation of the business.

c. LIMITED COMPANY

Many small businesses are organized as limited companies. The limited company, unlike the proprietorship and partnership, is a separate legal entity, with its own rights and duties, that can continue as a separate organization even after the death of an owner.

A limited company can be created for any size of business; it is wrong to consider it appropriate only for larger companies.

Establishing a limited company is both more complex and more costly (from a legal and accounting point of view) than

establishing a proprietorship or a partnership but, despite these problems, is an effective way of operating a business.

For regulatory purposes, a limited company is like a person. It can sue and be sued, just like an individual, and it must conform to regulatory authorities. A limited company is an ongoing organization with an infinite life of its own even though employees and owners come and go. Many of its assets, such as land and buildings, may indeed have a longer life than the life of the shareholders.

1. Public versus private companies

Limited companies may be established as either public or private. A public company is generally one that has its shares listed on a stock exchange. The legal requirements for operating a public company are much more strict than those for a private company. However, you will more likely be interested in organizing a private limited company since that type of company is designed for the small business operator.

A private company is one that is:

(a) restricted in its right to transfer shares,

(b) limited to a maximum number of shareholders, and

(c) prohibited from offering its shares to the public.

The regulations governing private corporations change from time to time. Consult your lawyer about the current requirements when you want to incorporate.

2. Incorporation

Companies can be incorporated in a single province or state, in one or more provinces or states, or federally. Since you will probably start out by operating your business in a single location, you need to incorporate only in that jurisdiction and then register in other jurisdictions as required.

You can have a lawyer set up the limited company for you or, in many cases, you can do this for yourself since books are available that show you, step by step, how this is done.

Doing it yourself may save you several hundred dollars. However, if the situation is complex, professional legal advice should be sought. For example, depending on your personal financial situation, there may be advantages to establishing the share structure of the company one way rather than another.

3. Advantages of incorporating

The major advantage of the limited company form of business is that, generally speaking, since the company is a separate legal entity, the individual owners cannot be held responsible for the company's liabilities. The owners, in other words, have a liability limited to their investment in shares in the company.

However, despite this, lending institutions that you approach for financing usually make you sign a personal note to extend your liability outside the protection offered by the company. This is particularly true for a new business.

Another advantage is that financing may be facilitated by the creation of easily transferable certificates of ownership, known as shares, that may be bought by or sold to others, including employees of the company.

This broadens the base of financing available to the company. The limited liability of share ownership appeals to some investors since it permits ownership, with a potential return on the investment, without involvement in the company's day-to-day operations.

There may also be some personal tax advantages to forming a limited company that make that form of business appealing. Since each situation is different, you should consult your accountant for the tax

pros and cons of forming a limited company that suits your particular personal situation.

4. Disadvantages of incorporating

Some disadvantages of the limited company are as follows.

Depending on its size and number of owners, decision making can be a lengthy process. Dilution of control and profits can also occur if there are a great many shareholders (although this would not normally be true of the typical private limited company).

Also, double taxation exists for shareholders of limited companies. The corporation pays taxes on its profit at the corporate tax rate. Any after-tax income may be distributed to the individual shareholders as dividends. The individual is then taxed on these dividends at personal tax rates.

A limited company is also subject to more government regulation and form remittance than a proprietorship or a partnership, although this is a small price to pay considering the advantages that incorporation may offer.

5. "S" corporations (U.S.)

Federal income taxes have an important and decided impact on the legal form of organization. Sometimes it is preferable for a proprietorship or partnership to become incorporated, at other times it is not. Since this can be a very complex subject, individual situations must be investigated on their own merits and the advice of a tax accountant considered.

In the U.S., however, you do have a tax option known as an "S" corporation. The philosophy behind the "S" corporation provisions of the internal revenue code is that a business should be able to choose its organizational form free of tax considerations. In essence, this type of corporation allows the business to operate with the highly advantageous limited liability for its owners, but without the corporate penalty of double taxation mentioned earlier, since an "S" corporation pays tax like a partnership.

To qualify, a corporation must

(a) have no more than 35 stockholders,

(b) be a domestic corporation, and

(c) have only one class of stock.

These qualifications change from time to time and it would be wise to discuss the "S" corporation form of business with your tax advisor before making any decision.

d. LEGAL FORM AND SALE OF BUSINESS

Finally, give some thought, even when starting out, to eventual sale or disposition of your business. This is something you should discuss with your accountant and lawyer since it can affect the legal form of business you initially set up, the income taxes you may have to pay when you retire and sell your business, or when the business passes to your heirs upon your death. (See *Buying and Selling a Small Business*, another title in the Self-Counsel Series.)

5
FINDING A SITE

Once you have settled on the type of business you wish to have, the product(s) and services it will handle, and the organizational form it will have, you then need to find a suitable site.

In this chapter, it is assumed that the general location of your business has been selected. Location, in this sense, means you have made a decision about the community or area in which you wish to do business, and that you are now down to the choice of a specific site within that location.

a. RUNNING A BUSINESS FROM YOUR HOME

In certain types of small retail businesses, it may be appropriate to operate out of your home. This is particularly true in some types of service businesses, such as an accounting or consulting firm, or for a mail order business.

Operating a small business out of your residence is not much different from operating out of an office or a shop, and it offers the following advantages:

(a) You avoid traffic problems and save money by reducing your traveling time.

(b) As well as being allowed to deduct expenses that relate specifically to the business part of your home (for example, plants and pictures) you can claim a portion of your general home expenses (depreciation, mortgage interest, maintenance, property taxes, and insurance) as a business expense.

Since what you can deduct depends on the individual circumstances, you should consult your accountant about this, particularly with reference to the pros and cons of claiming part of the building depreciation as a business deduction. Remember, however, that if you do run a business from your home, you will still probably need a business license.

b. IMPORTANCE OF SITE

If you do not plan to start a business that you can operate from your home, then site selection can be critical. The objective in site selection is to find a spot that will bring in the greatest number of customers at the lowest cost.

Sites are often selected because of their proximity to where the business owner lives or because the premises happen to be vacant or the price attractive. Don't fall into this trap unless you have subjected the site to some suitability tests.

A practical general rule is to select a site that suits the needs of the customers who are the market for the business. You should become familiar with the specifics of the business you are interested in to understand its particular site and market requirements.

Generally, since in retailing the customer has to come to your location, parking and/or public transportation should be convenient to your site.

1. Site specialists

If you are unfamiliar with the market requirements of your particular business, you may want to approach a site specialist. The services of site selection companies include analysis of population density, customer profiles, access and traffic flows, the drawing power of other businesses in the area, visibility of business and signs, the average sale you should have based on square feet, and what effect any nearby present or future competitors will have. Note, though, that assessing a commercial site is both complex and tricky. It is more art than science, and even the specialists can be wrong.

2. Some guidelines

Even though you may rely on a site specialist to help with site selection, there are some obvious things that you should be aware of. For example, don't locate in an area populated or frequented by people of a different socio-economic base than those you must sell your products or services to.

Similarly, you would not want to have a particular type of restaurant in an area that is populated with people whose ethnic background is not oriented to the type of food you will be selling; or locate a business geared to selling to the younger generation in an area inhabited by older married couples; or locate a high fashion clothing store next to a pinball machine shop.

A good retail site is frequently one near another store that is successfully attracting the kind of people you need as a market base. Sometimes a difference of 20 or 30 feet in site can have a drastic impact on sales, one way or another.

This is particularly true of shopping center or shopping mall sites. For example, if you are selling impulse items in a shopping mall, a location close to the main traffic flow at the entrance to a major department store, or by an escalator, is better than at the end of a corridor that is relatively quiet.

For some types of businesses, corner sites are most suitable since there are two

streams of pedestrian and/or vehicular traffic.

If your business is a unique one, such as a picture framing or watch repair store, location may not be as important since people in the community will seek you out because you have no competition. If this is your case, you can locate in a low rent and low traffic area.

However, if your business is more competitive (such as a grocery store) then traffic flow and pedestrian counts are more important.

c. VISIBILITY, ACCESSIBILITY, AND SUITABILITY

Three extremely important aspects of a good site are visibility, accessibility, and suitability. Each of these will be briefly discussed.

1. Visibility

Visibility of the business may be more important to the customer who arrives at your front door by automobile than it is for the pedestrian, but even for the pedestrian visibility is important.

Poor visibility of a business outlet can be improved by appropriate outdoor signs that can both attract attention and give directions. This is especially true in a site where the business is surrounded by larger and taller buildings, or where one-way streets and other complications can confuse the customer traveling by car.

2. Accessibility

A second factor in site location is accessibility, again particularly for those arriving by automobile. An ideal situation is where traffic flow in and around the site minimizes the effects of such things as left turn restrictions that prevent the motorist from easily approaching the business.

Equally important is knowledge about future street or highway changes that could change a desirable access situation into an undesirable one.

If a route from the main travel stream is difficult, and sign ordinances prohibit providing the motorist with information such as where to turn to reach the business, then a large number of potential customers may be lost.

3. Suitability

Even with good visibility and easy access, the suitability of the site is a critical factor. For many businesses, such as restaurants, motels, or building supply outlets, the greatest site limitation is space for parking. The space required for parking is usually greater than that required for the building.

If you are looking for land on which to erect a building, you need answers to the following questions:

(a) Is the site suitable for building expansion? For example, is it reasonably flat and free of rock outcroppings that might be expensive to remove or build around?

(b) Is road frontage adequate?

(c) Is there sufficient soil depth for the building so that large quantities of fill are not required?

Even if you don't have enough money now to buy more land than you need immediately, it might be a good idea to select a site with adjacent land that could be available for purchase for future building expansion.

d. LOCATION FACTORS

With retail and service businesses, size of population and number of competitors in the local trading area can be key considerations in finding a good site.

Many studies have been conducted to show the general surrounding population needed to support different types of retail/service businesses. For example, each grocery store might need a population of 800 to 1,000, whereas a store specializing in photography supplies and equipment might need a population base of 40,000.

These population ratios can vary from location to location. Visit the local trade association for the type of business you are planning to start to see what information they have. Your local Chamber of Commerce or Board of Trade may also be very helpful.

You should do your research and determine the population base for the particular type of business you are interested in. Measure this against the number of competitors you have to see if there is enough business for all of you.

Some further questions that you might like to answer concerning site specifics follow.

(a) Is the site suitable with regard to your competition?

(b) Is it in a high traffic area and are neighboring stores doing a good business?

(c) Will the demand for your products and/or services grow at that location?

(d) If the product(s) or service(s) are new, are they needed in that location or could another competitor in a better location survive, to your detriment?

(e) If the competition is currently inefficient or unaggressive, what impact would an improvement in their efficiency or aggressiveness do to this site?

(f) If parking is required, is it adequate and conveniently accessible?

(g) If location on a particular side of the street is important, is your potential site on the best side?

(h) Are there any disadvantages to this site? In other words, is there a more suitable site within this general area? For example, if the site is located between a used car lot and a take-out restaurant, would it be a good spot for a plant shop?

(i) Is the market a stable or growing one? Consider population trends, payrolls, and local attitudes.

(j) Is the site dependent on a seasonal business (for example, tourism)?

(k) In rented premises is it a high or low rent area?

(l) Is the rent competitive?

(m) If it is a low rent area and your competition is in a high rent area because of a more suitable site, how are you going to compensate for the relatively poorer location to attract business?

(n) Are the surrounding buildings in good repair? If they aren't, they may detract from your business.

(o) Is the area safe from vandals and is there good police and fire protection?

(p) Is there sufficient floor space and room for possible expansion?

(q) Can purchased products be easily delivered?

(r) If your customers will have to rely on public transportation, is it adequate and are there stops nearby?

e. DOWNTOWN AND SHOPPING CENTERS

You might also want to compare the pros and cons of a downtown location or a shopping center or mall.

1. Downtown

In a downtown area there are generally more potential customers among those working in the area. However, what is critical is whether or not these potential customers can be part of your market. If not, then your market must be from people outside the area who come to shop, in which case traffic and parking considerations are critical.

Also, in a downtown area you can expect major competition from large retail and department stores. Rent and operating costs will be higher as well.

Downtown locations are often not good for evening and Saturday business since suburban dwellers usually prefer to visit their local shopping malls rather than drive downtown.

2. Major shopping centers

Major shopping or community centers are distinguished from local shopping malls. Shopping centers serve communities of anywhere between 20,000 to 200,000 people, and are generally between a 10- and 40-minute drive from them.

Whether to locate in a major shopping center is a difficult decision. Shopping centers have high rents, but they do generally attract plenty of traffic and potential customers and have good accessibility, plenty of parking, pooled advertising possibilities, and potential for future business growth.

The lead store in a shopping center is usually a department store or supermarket. In the larger centers, there are two such department stores or supermarkets — one at either end. Prime locations are adjacent to one of these large stores, or at least between them, to ensure the best traffic flow.

Shopping centers also have the advantage of being located in a particular area as a result of extensive research by the center developer. However, you must be sure a shopping center is the right location for your type of business.

Shopping centers generally base part of their rent on your sales volume. For this reason they seek businesses with a potential for high sales volume and charge a high rent that is sometimes only affordable by chain or national companies. New, untested businesses without any special features to attract more people to the center are often discouraged by shopping center managers because such businesses have a low or non-existent credit rating.

In addition, in shopping centers you may also have to pay a monthly flat fee, or a percentage of your sales, for general shopping center advertising. In some cases, this fee is based on the square foot area of your business. If so, check to see how much is added to your premises' actual square foot area as your share of "common" areas. You might be unpleasantly surprised.

Check also to see if there is a shopping center merchants' association and whether or not all tenants must join. If so, find out how much the membership fee is going to add to your payments.

Remember also, in most shopping centers your hours of operation and other rules are more or less dictated to you. Find out in advance what they are and decide whether or not you can live with them.

3. Neighborhood shopping malls

Neighborhood shopping malls serve local populations from 5,000 to 20,000 people and are either within walking distance or a few minutes' drive from the majority of that population.

Your market is generally limited to the population living in the immediate area and because parking is often a problem you may have to rely on walk-in trade. Not all products or services are suited to that. On the other hand, rent and other costs may be lower.

f. BYLAWS AND SIMILAR PROBLEMS

Before going too far with starting a business on what seems a desirable site, it is best to make sure that all the local bylaws such as zoning restrictions, building codes, fire regulations, and similar laws will allow you to operate your type of business there. For the same reason, check out any necessary licensing or certification for your type of business.

1. Zoning

Zoning regulates such matters as size of structure, the portion of a lot that may have a building on it, proximity to street, parking requirements, the use to which a building may be put, the size and type of outdoor sign permitted, and even population density in the area that may/or may not allow your type of business. If you have any doubts, check first with your local government's planning/zoning department.

If zoning does not allow a larger building on the site, or if there are such problems as height restrictions, can a change in zoning (a variance) be obtained from the local government? Your lawyer can be very helpful in zoning matters.

Parking can also be a problem. Find out if there is any minimum parking space requirement for your type of business.

Sign ordinances should also be checked to determine if there are any restrictions on type, placement, number, and size of signs.

Make sure that the information obtained concerning bylaws and ordinances is up to date since changes do occur in these regulations from time to time.

2. Utilities

A check with the local engineering or public works department will provide information about the present suitability of sewers, water mains, and electrical power supplies. If these are not adequate for the size of building planned, the cost to upgrade them could be prohibitive.

The proximity of connection points for utility services is also important since the cost could be exorbitant for extra hookups to one or more of these services that might be several hundred yards away.

3. Highways

Ask the highways department to provide information concerning their future plans for new highways or bypass routes that could severely affect the visibility and accessibility of your business.

For example, if the business is on a two-lane highway that is slated for widening to four lanes, is a divider planned for separating the two halves of the highway? If this is the case, it may make if difficult, if not impossible, for arriving or departing motorists to drive directly into or out of the property.

If a purchase of land is involved, the land deed should be checked to see what easements or other restrictions there are. Are there any buildings on the land that will first have to be demolished? If so, the cost of demolition must be added to the asking price for the land.

4. Property appraisal

Before making the final commitment to purchase a building, or building and land, for your business, an appraisal is recommended. This appraisal will allow you to compare the site selected with information about similar properties in the area. If necessary, obtain a second appraisal for confirmation. The money invested in this ensures that the business is not located on an overpriced, unsuitable site.

g. SUMMARY

In selecting a site, observe the situation, talk to other merchants in the area, and check for any increasing trend of bankruptcies in the general area. Find out if there is a local merchants' association. If there is, attend one or two meetings to find out the concerns of local merchants and see who their leaders are so that you can talk to them.

Selecting the right site involves skill, common sense, knowledge, good judgment, and an awareness of the requirements of a successful business (e.g., traffic patterns and circulation, business generators, building planning, real estate, and luck in site selection).

6
BUILDING CONSTRUCTION

If you plan to rent the premises for your retail store, you might wish to skip this chapter concerning construction of a building. However, there are some items in the section on pre-opening schedule that apply equally well to opening a business in leased premises.

Normally, when you are starting a new retail business, you should not consider buying land for constructing a new building or buying an existing building. In fact, some lenders of money will not lend it to those new to retailing for such purposes.

However, there may be exceptions. For example, to establish a franchised business, the franchisor may insist that you own a freestanding building. In such situations, the franchisor ought to be able to provide the financing, or help in finding financing.

Generally, most first-time business retailers invest far too much money in bricks and mortar (the building) when they should be leasing that asset, particularly in the early years. To a lesser degree the same is true of equipment and fixtures.

It is in these early years that the risk is often the greatest, and you may not be able to afford the heavy mortgage debt load that owning land and/or a building and expensive equipment carries.

However, if your new retail business requires that you construct a building, some detailed costing will be required so that your financial plan (see chapter 9) can be more accurately prepared.

a. CONSTRUCTION COST

If the land has to be purchased prior to construction, the cost of this land should be a known amount. Don't forget to add to it any costs involved in preparing the site for construction, and possibly even landscaping costs.

The cost of constructing the building must then be estimated. One of the most useful methods of estimating cost is based on the cost of construction per square foot for that type of building in that locality at the present time.

The total square foot requirements are simply multiplied by the current cost per square foot. The total cost may have to be adjusted upward for special features of the building that might increase its basic construction cost. For example, the cost of an elevator if the building is two or more stories high would substantially increase the cost.

If a more detailed costing is desired for land and building, a form such as that illustrated in Sample #1 is useful.

When the total estimated cost of the site and building has been calculated, add to this total an estimate of architect and other consultants' fees, plus a reserve for contingencies of 10% to 20%.

This contingency is necessary to take care of actual costs that exceed estimates, of extras that are not anticipated, and building changes that are not perceived until the building is well underway.

SAMPLE #1
BREAKDOWN OF SITE AND BUILDING COSTS

GENERAL	$_____	BROUGHT FORWARD	$_____
Permits, plans, surveys	$_____	FINISHES:	$_____
Fees	$_____	Millwork	$_____
		Floors	$_____
SITE:		Ceilings	$_____
Land purchase	$_____	Furnishings	$_____
		Labor	$_____
SITE WORK:			
Clearing	$_____	ELECTRICAL:	
Services: Sewer	$_____	Wiring	$_____
Water	$_____	Fixtures	$_____
Excavation	$_____	Other	$_____
Fill	$_____	Labor	$_____
Paving and/or gravel	$_____		
Landscaping	$_____	PLUMBING:	
Fencing	$_____	Materials	$_____
Labor	$_____	Labor	$_____
CONCRETE:		HEATING:	
Footings	$_____	Materials	$_____
Foundations	$_____	Labor	$_____
Reinforcing	$_____		
Floors	$_____	PAINTING:	
Labor	$_____	Materials	$_____
		Labor	$_____
WALLS:			
Concrete blocks	$_____	HARDWARE:	
Masonry	$_____	Materials	$_____
Woodwork	$_____	Labor	$_____
Partitions	$_____		
Drywall	$_____	OTHER ITEMS:	
Sheeting	$_____	Air-conditioning	$_____
Insulation	$_____	Elevators	$_____
Labor	$_____	Sprinkler	$_____
		Sign	$_____
WALL OPENINGS:			
Doors	$_____		
Windows	$_____		
Ventilation	$_____		
Labor	$_____		
ROOF:			
Materials	$_____		
Labor	$_____		
		TOTAL COST	$_____
CARRIED FORWARD	$_____		

b. CHOICE OF CONSTRUCTION APPROACH

With design plans prepared and specifications approved by local authorities, a choice must then be made concerning the method to use for construction coordination. You can employ a general contractor, or a project supervisor or manager, or supervise the job yourself.

Regardless of which method is selected, responsibility for supervision of the contractor's work should be left to the architect and the consultants who have been employed. This ensures that building construction is carried out within the terms and conditions of the contract (more about this later).

However, the diversity of types of contracts should be discussed with the architect who, because of his or her profession, is familiar with them. This discussion should take place at an early stage in the development of the working drawings since any subsequent changes can considerably affect the construction time schedule and related problems.

1. General contractor

A common method of construction is to employ a general contractor. This process begins with contractors submitting bids or tenders on the entire building construction after they have had an opportunity to review the building specifications.

These tenders can be open to all contractors, or they can be closed or limited to those contractors known for their high quality construction standards. The contractor's price includes labor, material, and supervisory costs, plus the contractor's own profit.

Control over a contractor is achieved through bonding. Two types of bond are common. A bid bond means that the contractor guarantees that construction will start when specified in the tender. A performance bond provides you with funds to complete the building if the contractor runs into difficulties and cannot fulfill the contract.

The construction contract can also include penalty clauses, such as one that requires the contractor to pay you a specified sum of money if construction is incomplete by a stated date. Contracts with construction companies should always be reviewed by your lawyer before they are signed.

When a contractor puts in a bid, costs should be detailed. The contractor's fee is usually about 10% of the total building cost. For this the contractor obtains all permits, supervises and pays all tradespeople, purchases and pays for all materials (including shipping charges), coordinates all the various subcontractors, and guarantees the finished building.

There should be no "extras" unless they have been agreed to. This might occur if the contractor was unable to obtain a price at the time the bid was made. In such cases, some protection against exorbitant costs for that possibility should be built into the contract.

Also, it is possible that you might change some item of design during construction and this could change the final construction costs.

2. Project supervisor

An alternative to hiring a general contractor is to have a project supervisor or manager negotiate with you and your architect for the construction of the project.

In such a case, the project supervisor is responsible for tendering and hiring the subtrades, and then supervising them. You are responsible for purchasing all construction materials and paying the tradespeople involved, and the project supervisor or manager simply receives a fee for supervisory responsibilities.

One advantage of this method is that the architect may issue certain drawings in sequence, permitting an early start on construction before total completion of all working drawings and specifications.

With this approach you must be careful to establish a maximum allowable building construction cost. The project supervisor, or better still the architect or you, should use the services of a qualified surveyor or building estimator to establish the probable maximum total building construction cost and to ensure a system of continuing cost control.

3. Owner supervised construction

Another alternative is for you to supervise construction. This eliminates the profit of the general contractor, or the fee of the project supervisor, but adds considerably to the demands on your time. Unless you have considerable experience in construction, this route is not recommended.

If you do handle the construction yourself, you should commit the estimated costs involved to paper. A useful form for this is shown in Sample #1. It would be wise to complete this form before construction starts to obtain a relatively firm idea of what is involved in total outlay for construction.

c. CONTRACT DETAILS

Regardless of which construction approach is taken, a formal contract should be drawn up. Apart from defining the legal implications of the contract, such as stating the names of the supervisory architect, building owner, and contractor, the contract should spell out at least the following contractor responsibilities:

(a) Supervision and construction procedures

(b) Cost control of labor and materials

(c) Warranty responsibilities for permits, fees, notices, taxes, and cash allowances

(d) Responsibilities of work superintendent and other employees

(e) Preparation of progress schedules

(f) Maintaining drawings and specifications on the building site so they will be available to you

(g) Channels for communication

(h) Site cleanup

(i) Procedures for claims for damages

(j) Your rights upon default of the contractor

(k) Contract fee payment amount and methods, including circumstances warranting withholdings for non-performance

(l) Final payment for work completion

(m) Construction insurance requirements and responsibilities

(n) Contract termination by either party

This is only a "bare bones" list to indicate some of the important considerations to be included in a construction contract. It is not intended to be all-inclusive, but only to point out some of the many considerations involved in construction of a new building. Consultation with a lawyer is imperative when drawing up construction contracts.

d. INSURANCE

An important consideration during construction is to protect money that is invested in the building as it is constructed. This protection is handled by insurance.

Indeed, before construction even begins, you would be wise to study the many comprehensive multiple line protection policies offered by insurance companies competitive in the field.

The basic type of insurance coverage required is for loss to building(s) and personal property on a stipulated peril basis (such as fire, lightning, and earthquake). In addition, consider optional coverage such as sprinkler leakage, vandalism, malicious mischief, and public liability.

Generally, building insurance covers all permanent fixtures (including such items as heating, cooling, air-conditioning, elevators, and similar engineering and/or mechanical equipment) as well as signs attached to the building. As building

29

construction progresses, the insurance policy should provide for periodic automatic increases in the building insurance amount.

e. PRE-OPENING SCHEDULE

Since the construction time for any particular building can vary because of factors such as size and type of construction, the following schedule is only a rough guide to the steps involved and their timing prior to opening.

1. One to two years before opening

During this period preliminary architectural drawings should be completed and local planning authorities contacted to ensure that design and construction practices do not violate basic planning guidelines and regulatory requirements. In addition, electrical and mechanical engineers should be engaged to provide the design of, or design advice on, such items as electrical systems, heating and plumbing, air-conditioning, and possibly elevators.

2. One to one-and-one-half years before opening

Searching and applying for financing must begin. Construction tenders should be called for — this usually takes about a month. If interior designers and landscape architects are to be used, their services should be contracted for during this period. Final design work for the building should also be completed now.

This final design should be approved by all necessary local government agencies or authorities so that a building permit can be applied for. If an interior designer is to be used, he or she should produce final drawings and specifications for fixtures, furniture, and equipment so that tenders can be called.

3. One year before opening

About a year before opening, construction should be well on the way, or at least have been started. An office should be set up on the site with a telephone. A mailing address, with the business's name, should be established with the post office. It is at this time that your preliminary marketing plan should be started (see chapter 8).

Pre-opening expenses must be estimated to ensure that funds will be available to pay for them.

4. Six months before opening

Product prices should be established. The opening date should be fairly definitely set, and any advertising campaign planned (radio, newspapers, and any other media).

5. Three to six months before opening

Begin the search for any key employees to be hired. If service contracts are to be arranged for any necessary equipment, they should be signed.

6. One month before opening

By now the opening date should be finalized. Key employees should have been hired and final decisions made on which applicants for jobs are to be hired. Key employees should supervise the installation of any necessary fixtures and equipment. They should have prepared lists of necessary operating supplies so that these can be ordered and delivered prior to opening.

7. One to three weeks before opening

All staff should be on the premises for training and orientation and so that dry runs can be carried out on inventory location, equipment usage, and service procedures. These dry runs will help test all the facilities. If there are any problems with equipment not working properly and similar matters they can be detected and corrected prior to the arrival of the first customers.

f. PLANNING OPENING DATE

The opening date of your new business should be carefully planned. When constructing premises, this can be difficult, since there can be construction holdups for any number of reasons, and planned and actual opening dates could be months apart.

However, when leasing premises, you should keep the nature of your business very much in mind when agreeing to a starting date before signing a lease. Many businesses are seasonal (for example, a sporting goods store) and many have other peaks and valleys (for example, for many businesses the Christmas season accounts for as much as 30% of total annual sales). If you open such a business in the "off" season you may have many months of struggle until you have adequate cash flow.

In other words, you must understand the nature of your business and try to open it at the best time of year for sales.

g. YELLOW PAGES

Another factor to keep in mind when planning your opening is a listing in the Yellow Pages of the telephone book.

Most small retail businesses rely heavily on Yellow Page telephone directory advertising to both take away customers from competitive stores, and to attract new customers.

Yellow Page directories are printed and distributed only once a year, and deadlines for a listing can be several months before that. Find out deadline and distribution dates for your locality. Make sure you have a listing in the year you open and, better still, try to plan your opening at or about the time the new Yellow Pages is issued.

If it is issued in June without your listing and you open in July, you are going to have 11 months of struggle and extra advertising costs to make yourself known.

7
RENTING PREMISES AND EQUIPMENT

As a retailer, chances are you will start your new business in leased or rented premises. Generally, most first-time business owners invest far too much money in bricks and mortar (the building) when they should be leasing that asset, particularly in the early days. To a lesser degree, the same is true of equipment and fixtures.

In these early years, the risk is often the greatest, and you may not be able to afford the heavy mortgage debt load that owning land and/or a building and expensive equipment carry. Many leases can be arranged that allow you a later purchase option.

a. LAND AND BUILDING LEASE

A lease is basically a partnership agreement between the landlord (the owner of the land and/or building) and the tenant (the operator of the building).

There is invariably a very direct relationship between the amount of rent charged for retail business premises and the pedestrian or traffic count — the higher the count the higher the rent.

However, a low rent location can sometimes be overcome by spending more on advertising. But if the amount spent on advertising is greater than the rent savings, there is obviously no net benefit in choosing that location.

If your business is such that the customer must find you, you should rent premises that are easy to find and easy to reach.

When checking out premises for possible rent, do more than look at the space and determine how large the square foot area is. Check to see if the walls, floor, and ceiling are finished and if not find out who pays to put the premises in rentable condition.

Some premises, even in shopping centers, are rented as bare leases. Premises rented this way are referred to as "shells." Generally, the utilities are brought only to the wall (stubbed in). You pay for all inside finishing, even down to light fixtures, plumbing, window coverings, and heating, and air-conditioning equipment. Determine in advance what this is going to cost so that there are no unhappy surprises later.

It is normal that any special inside finishing is your responsibility. However, if you are going to do any extensive internal remodelling that would subsequently be of benefit to the landlord when your lease expires, see if you can negotiate a reduced rent because of this.

1. Lease agreements

There is no standard commercial lease agreement. Each lease agreement must be prepared by the lawyers of the two parties involved depending on the particular circumstances of the situation.

The agreement should cover such matters as the length of the contract (for example, 5, 10, or even 20 or more years), the amount of rent and frequency of payment, the responsibility of the two parties for the maintenance of the property, and who pays which costs for items such as major maintenance (plumbing, electrical, air-conditioning) or minor maintenance

32

(cleaning and cleaning supplies), and other items such as building alterations, property taxes, and insurance.

Because of the ever-escalating cost of land and property development, property taxes, maintenance, and upgrading, a landlord will try to make rental periods as short as possible to ensure that rental rates high enough to cover all his or her costs can be negotiated more frequently. Your objective, of course, is just the reverse. From your perspective, an initial lease of 15 years with two five-year renewal options would be desirable but may not be achievable without difficult negotiations. A long initial lease period allows you to spread your investment costs over more years.

2. Expense pass-throughs

Some lease contracts contain expense pass-throughs. In other words, some of the landlord's "normal" expenses are now the responsibility of the tenant. The most common pass-through is known as a triple net lease in which the tenant pays for all maintenance, property taxes, and building insurance. This can have a double effect. Any remodeling you do (such as building improvements) increases the value of the building and will thus increase your property taxes, even though you don't own the building!

Similarly, businesses in the area may be assessed a special property tax for improved community lighting, sewers, or other works. As a tenant under triple net, you will pay that added burden.

Read the contract carefully, and have your lawyer go over it since some leases state that if you attach anything to floors, walls, or ceilings it becomes the property of the lessor. This means that you could invest several thousand dollars in shelving, special lighting, equipment fixed to the floor, and so on, and as soon as you install it it is no longer legally yours.

3. Restrictions

Check the contract carefully to see if there are any restrictions on your business operations by the landlord or others, such as any conditions or restrictions on subletting, which you may want to do if the business is not successful and your lease still has some time to run.

The landlord should not have the right to unreasonably withhold your right to sublet, assign, or mortgage your lease, or even sell it for its remaining life, including options (see below) to someone else. If your business is successful, the right to sell its goodwill for a profit can be quite valuable to you.

Measure your floor space so that if rent is based on square footage, you will not be charged for more space than you have. However, note that in some shopping malls "your" space includes a share of common areas such as halls, storage areas, elevators, etc. Find out in advance what your share of this common space is.

4. Renewal option

An initial relatively short contract with one or more renewal options is often preferable to a long-term lease contract. Renewal options prevent you from being locked in if the business is not successful, but allow you to continue if it is a profitable enterprise. Any renewal options and their terms should be written into the initial contract.

In older buildings in a city core, landlords may be very reluctant to include options since they never know when an offer may come along from an investor wishing to tear down the building and construct a new one. Your successful business with two or three renewals could be an obstacle for the landlord.

Regarding renewal options, note that any change in rent rates should be negotiated for the new period near the end of the present lease term. If you have the right to a renewal term, it is important to give the landlord a renewal notice within the time frame stipulated in the contract. Otherwise, you might find that you lose your right to a renewal option.

5. Fixtures and equipment

The typical lease is generally only for the land and building, with the lessee (or tenant) purchasing and owning the fixtures and equipment.

If the equipment and similar items are owned by the landlord (in which case the lease payments will generally be higher), the lease agreement should specify how frequently these items are to be replaced and at whose cost.

If the tenant owns the equipment and similar items, the lease contract should provide for the disposition of them at the end of the lease period.

The two most common arrangements are that the tenant is responsible for complete removal of such items at his or her cost, or that the landlord has the right to buy them at some stipulated value.

6. Contingencies

Make sure any necessary contingencies are in the contract. Contingencies might be that the contract depends on your request for a business license being approved, or that financing for purchasing equipment is obtained, or that all necessary government licenses, permits, and variances are approved. Finally, a contingency that you may inspect the site to check that it conforms to the lease description should be included.

7. Rental arrangements

With any form of lease operation, it is normal for the tenant to bear the burden of any operating losses, although, depending on the lease arrangement, some of the net profit may have to be shared with the landlord under certain circumstances.

There are a variety of rental arrangement possibilities with leasing. Some of these will be discussed.

(a) Fixed rental

A fixed rental arrangement calls for straight payments during the term of the lease. The payment might be a stepped one that increases, for example, year by year during the term of the lease. However, the payments are not variable with, and do not depend on, your sales or profits.

The lease agreement will probably allow renegotiation of the fixed amount of rent during the life of the agreement, particularly if the life is for an extended number of years.

If a fixed rental cost appears cheap when based on a dollar amount per square foot of leased space, do not be misled if it appears to be lower than the market rates. In other words, make sure that there are no "hidden" expenses.

(b) Variable rental

A variable rental has a fixed portion, usually at least sufficient to give the tenant cash flow to amortize loan obligations, cover expenses, and provide a return on investment. In addition, there is additional rent based either on your gross sales or on your net profit.

The variable rent portion gives the landlord some hedge against inflation, although there might be a ceiling rent amount stated in the contract.

(c) Percentage of sales

Another possibility is for rent to be based on sales. If so, what is to be included in sales should be completely spelled out. For example, is rental income from a part of the building subleased by you to a third party to be included in sales?

Most contracts allow for a declining percentage as sales increase. For example, rent may be 6% of sales up to a certain level, then decline to 5% for any sales above that level.

Some contracts call for an increasing percentage of sales as sales increase — an escalation clause. This can be risky for you since the accelerating percentage can seriously erode normal net profit margins as sales continue to climb.

(d) Percentage of net profit

With rent partly based on percentage of sales, the landlord is in a type of partnership arrangement with you. With the variable portion of rent based on net profit, this partnership becomes even more firm. The net profit must be carefully defined in the lease contract as either profit before income tax, profit before interest and tax, or profit before depreciation, interest, and tax.

In some lease contracts, to protect the landlord, the amount of certain types of expenses may be limited. For example, if your salary is not limited, you could pay yourself such an inflated amount that there would be no net profit to be shared with the landlord as rent.

In other cases, the contract may specify a minimum amount that you must spend each year for advertising, for example, so that sufficient sales and net profit are generated, or for maintenance so that the building is kept in good condition.

(e) Sale leaseback

One other type of lease arrangement is the sale leaseback. This occurs when a building owner sells the land to a land investor and agrees to lease it back for a number of years.

Alternatively, the owner may sell both land and the building to a property investor and contract to lease both of them back in order to be able to continue to operate the business.

A sale leaseback may also be advisable when you start a business in ideal premises but are unable to obtain a lease because the owner wishes to sell. You might be able to arrange in advance with a third party that, at the time the purchase of the building or building and land is concluded, these assets will be immediately sold to that third party under a leaseback arrangement to you.

The sale leaseback arrangement is also useful to a person already in business who wishes to buy another one. The cash freed up from the sale of the present land, or land and building, reduces the requirement to find financing for the new business.

Under some sale leaseback arrangements you may also be able to structure the contract so that, at the end of the lease period, you regain ownership of the building and/or land.

8. Other considerations

Note that rental terms quoted by a landlord are negotiable, even if the landlord tries to make you believe otherwise. For example, if the landlord wants you as a tenant, you may be able to negotiate that the landlord provide all improvements to meet the occupancy code for use of that space by your type of business and provide the required electrical, heating, ventilation, and air-conditioning systems.

Even at this early stage you should have a design firm involved in the process because they can provide appropriate advice about power and other needed services. Many landlords stipulate that you must use architects and/or designers in any remodeling of premises. Their cost can be surprisingly high.

Before signing any lease, make sure you have all area bylaw and zoning clearances, and preferably include in the lease a release clause protecting you against restrictions prohibiting your type of operation or affecting important operating practices. Also, confirm that "shell" packages have the necessary factors for your business's use such as fire-rated walls, sprinklers, appropriate entrance and exit doors, plumbing, and electrical services.

9. Advantages of leasing

There are a number of advantages to leasing.

(a) Under a lease arrangement you have the obvious advantage of not having to provide capital to buy the property. Any capital that you might have is then available for investment elsewhere.

(b) It also frees up your borrowing power to raise money, if required, for more critical areas of the business.

(c) Lease payments on a building are generally fully tax deductible. Also, whereas owned land is not depreciable for tax purposes, the cost of leasing it is tax deductible.

(d) Any leasehold improvements that you make to the building are generally amortized over the life of the lease rather than over the life of the building. The lease period will normally be less than the building life, therefore providing a tax saving.

(e) You may have a purchase option at the end of the lease period when it may be desirable to buy the land and/or building and you have the cash to do this.

(f) If and when the time comes to sell the business, it may be easier to do if there is no real estate involved.

(g) Although you would not normally have this in mind when entering a lease transaction, in case of unexpected bankruptcy you would probably only be liable for one year's rent rather than long-term mortgage payments on a property that you had purchased.

(h) Finally, it may be possible to arrange a lease with rental payments adjusted to the business's seasonal cash flows, even though total annual rent would be the same amount.

10. Disadvantages of leasing

Keep in mind these disadvantages of leasing.

(a) Any capital gain in the assets accrues to the landlord and not to you. In a similar way, at the expiry of the lease, the value of the future profit of the business that you have worked hard to build up does not benefit you unless the lease is renewed.

(b) The cost of a lease may be higher than some other forms of financing.

(c) It may also be more difficult for you to borrow money with leased premises if there are no assets (other than a lease agreement) to pledge as collateral.

(d) Finally, the total cash outflow in rental payments may be greater in the long run than for purchasing the property.

11. Rental agents

If you are negotiating a lease through a rental agent, remember that the agent has only one mandate: to rent empty space for the landlord as quickly as possible to earn a commission.

Remember that you know, or should know, more about what you want in the way of premises for your particular line of business than the agent does. In other words, be prepared by arming yourself in advance with as many facts as possible about the type and the size of premises you need.

Also, be alert to agents who show no interest in ensuring that you rent adequate premises, in a good location for your type of retailing.

b. EQUIPMENT LEASE

Consider also the possibility of leasing needed fixtures and equipment in order to minimize your start-up costs.

Most equipment leases cannot be canceled and require you to make a series of payments whose total sum will exceed the cost of assets if purchased outright, since the lessor has to make a profit on his or her investment.

Depreciation of the assets is the lessor's prerogative as owner of the assets. Maintenance is usually, but not invariably, a cost of the lessor.

Generally, the lessor owns any residual value in the assets, although contracts sometimes give you as lessee the right to purchase the assets at your option, at a specified price, at the end of the lease period. In such cases, the lease purchase is actually a type of conditional sale and you would have any tax advantages that claiming expenses such as depreciation may offer.

In some cases, you will also have the option to renew the lease for a specified period.

Some suppliers will lease equipment directly. In other cases, you lease from a company that specializes in leasing and that has bought the equipment from the supplier. The supplier may act as an intermediary in such cases.

1. Advantages of equipment leasing

Flexibility is an advantage of leasing equipment because you avoid the risk of obsolescence you might otherwise have if the assets are purchased outright. However, the lessor probably considers the cost of obsolescence when the lease rates are determined.

You also avoid the problems of maintenance and its cost. However, the lessor will normally build the cost of maintenance into the lease payments.

If there is no down payment required, 100% financing of leased assets may be possible. This has an advantage even if you have the cash to pay for such short-lived assets outright. This cash is then free for investment in longer-lived assets, such as land or building, that frequently appreciate in value as time goes by. Equipment depreciates very rapidly and usually has little or no residual value.

Finally, income tax is an important consideration. Since lease payments are generally fully tax deductible, there can be an advantage in leasing. On the other hand, ownership permits deduction for income tax purposes of both depreciation and the interest expense on any debt financing of the purchase. However, what might be advantageous with one lease arrangement may be disadvantageous with another. Each situation must be considered on its own merits as far as tax implications are concerned.

A sale leaseback of equipment is also not uncommon. You simply sell your equipment to a bank, finance company, or even a leasing firm at a price close to its current market value and then lease it back for its remaining usable life. However, the lease costs may be comparatively high since the lessor receives little or no tax benefit (for example, through depreciation) for owning used equipment. In addition, there may be sales or use taxes on the transaction.

2. Disadvantages of equipment leasing

A disadvantage of leasing equipment is that any money borrowed to make the lease payments can be more expensive by an interest point or more than money borrowed to purchase the equipment outright.

Also, the lessor is the owner of the equipment and has the right to repossess it if you do not meet the payments. If you owned the equipment, you would not lose any residual value remaining in it.

8
MARKET ANALYSIS

Every business must be concerned with its market. The word market is defined in terms of people, their money, and their desire to exchange it for goods and/or services.

A retailer's market is generally limited to a particular area, like a community or a town, and it may be further limited by competition, customers' preferences, or the availability of alternative goods or services.

Market analysis is based on the assumption that your business must be developed around the customers' wants and needs in order to satisfy those customers. Customers are, therefore, the reason for being in business.

It is the marketing process that will eventually determine whether or not your business is successful. Too many retailers ignore marketing to their detriment.

Marketing involves finding out what the user or consumer wants, designing products or services to meet these wants, analyzing existing products or services with reference to current user or consumer desires, determining the profit you want, establishing prices to achieve this profit, and creating and implementing an advertising/sales effort that will make users or consumers aware of your products or services and why they are desirable.

The ultimate objective is the satisfaction of the user or consumer at a profit to you. Too many small companies put the cart before the horse. They have products and then look for a market that they can create to sell them. In other words, the emphasis is on the need to sell the product rather than on the consumers' desires.

a. MARKET SURVEY

Before a new business offers any products, a market analysis or survey should be undertaken. This survey ultimately determines if a sales goal can be met and aids in financial planning (discussed in the next chapter).

A new retail business in a new area may have to carry out an extensive market survey. However, a new retail store in a well established shopping center where extensive market surveys have already been conducted may only need extensive advertising to introduce its business.

You may need to use specialists in market research to provide you with market information pertinent to your planned business and to develop a specific market forecast and action plan to serve that market.

1. Develop a questionnaire

In some cases, where you are going to be dealing primarily with the local pedestrian traffic, you might be able to design a simple questionnaire that you can administer yourself. It will provide you with information about your potential customers' needs.

A typical, simple questionnaire for a take-out restaurant is illustrated in Sample #2.

Since it would be physically impossible, and unnecessary, to survey the entire local population with your self-developed questionnaire, only a small segment of that market need be sampled. A good representative sample, in most cases, would be from 100 to 300 potential customers.

SAMPLE #2
MARKET ANALYSIS QUESTIONNAIRE
(Take-out restaurant)

1. If you use a take-out restaurant in this area, which one is it?_____

2. Why do you use that one?_____

3. Do you walk or drive there? _____

4. At what time of the day do you usually go there?_____

5. How often have you been there in the past month?_____year?_____

6. How do you rate that restaurant for

	Good	Average	Poor
Food quality	_____	_____	_____
Price	_____	_____	_____
Cleanliness	_____	_____	_____
Service	_____	_____	_____

7. In a new take-out restaurant in this area, what type of food would you like to see?_____

_____

8. In a new take-out restaurant in this area, what features would you like to see? _____

_____

9. Any other comments?_____

_____

_____

You could reach the sample by mailing out questionnaires, by interviewing on the telephone, or on the street.

The results of the questionnaires, once tabulated, should provide you with sufficient highlights to indicate the direction your business should be going and potential market size.

2. Traffic counts

In some situations, traffic counts (pedestrian and/or vehicular) can provide information on likely market size.

You might be able to obtain vehicular traffic counts from your local city hall engineering department. Alternatively, you can make the count yourself, but take counts at different times of day and different days of the week to obtain realistic averages.

Not all passers-by are potential customers. For example, pedestrians on their way to and from work may not be potential shoppers for your store, unless you are selling convenience or impulse items.

Similarly, if you plan to sell women's clothing, male pedestrians may not be of much interest to you, nor would older people if you were planning to sell records or tapes of music oriented to younger people.

39

3. General market survey

In other cases, a general market survey should be carried out to determine the limits of your market trading area. For example, a downtown trading area is geographically small, but potentially large as far as number of customers are concerned. On the other hand, a suburban neighborhood can be geographically spread out and a new retail business may be heavily dependent on driving distance.

A useful device is to draw concentric circles from your location to the population centers around you and add up how many people live within each distance/time of driving zone. Remember also that distance, for some retail businesses, can mean delivery expense.

Within each geographical boundary for your business you must determine population and competition. Each successful retail business can only be supported by a given number of people.

For example, if a trading area with a population of 40,000 can only support two retail stores of your type, and there are already two in business you would have to seriously consider whether a third could survive.

Alternatively, if the two stores already there are surviving only marginally because of poor management or other reasons, you could possibly move in and take away sufficient business to thrive.

If you are going to compete in a market that is successfully filled by other retailers, you may have a problem. It is best if you can find a gap that is not being filled by others. Ask yourself what unique products or services you can offer that differ from what others are offering.

Your general market survey should provide you with answers to the following typical questions:

(a) What is the market size?

(b) Is it growing?

(c) What is the market's geographical distribution?

(d) What share of the market can you obtain?

(e) What products or services is it interested in?

(f) Why is it interested in these goods or services?

(g) What price is it prepared to pay?

(h) How frequently does it buy?

(i) How will you provide the market with information about your products?

Effective marketing depends on the answers to these questions for your general trading area.

b. MARKET SEGMENT

The questions above are very broad in nature and need to be refined to produce more specific information that allows market segmentation. In other words, it is unlikely an individual firm will sell to a broad range of possible users or customers.

The product that you sell has a major impact in determining who your customers will be. For example, a specialized product will be purchased by a narrower segment of the market than a more general item.

1. Quality

Quality of product can also play a role. A work wear clothing store will cater to a different segment of the population than a store whose prime product is men's dress clothing. But even in men's clothing there are different markets — from those who wish a low priced rack suit through to those who wish only custom tailored clothing.

2. Price

Price is also a factor in market segmentation and can, to a degree, dictate the market segment you are dealing with. But price alone may not be the only significant factor since a higher price for a similar product, combined with better service, can also appeal to a special market segment that is not interested in having to inform itself.

Alternatively, there are those who are looking for low priced goods and for whom quality is not very relevant. In other cases, knowing that you are dealing with the large budget market, you may be able to buy quality goods in large quantities and sell them since your price can be lowered to the market segment that you normally deal with.

3. Basics versus nonbasics

Your market can also be segmented into major products that are necessities (such as food and clothing) versus nonbasic and/or impulse items (such as sportswear or gourmet foods).

4. Competition

Existing competition may also dictate the market segment that you must concentrate on. For example, if the area you choose for a high fashion store is already well served by firmly established high fashion stores, you may have to aim your store toward a lower priced market. The reverse is also true.

Alternatively, if there is already competition in the market you wish to serve, perhaps you can still enter that market by differentiating your products and/or services sufficiently (for example, through pricing economies or better service) and earn a profitable share of that market.

5. Defining your segment

You must identify and select those types of buyers with different needs within the broad market and then specifically select those you wish to serve. This segmentation can be based on geographic differences (e.g., proximity to the customers to be served), demographic differences (sex, income, occupation, education, age, family size, social class), or psychographic differ-

ences (lifestyle, user or consumer status, loyalty, etc.).

6. Use census figures

Census figures can often provide useful information to help you in market segmentation. Census figures can even be narrowed down to your immediate area and provide information and trends such as:

(a) The number of persons or families

(b) What proportion of the people are homeowners or renters

(c) The average family income

(d) The number of new single family homes built in that area over the last five years

(e) The number of people employed away from their homes

(f) The number of men or women in different age groups

(g) The average number of automobiles per family

(h) The number of appliances per home

Study the census information in your trading area for possible sales characteristics. Size of population may not always be relevant. Trend of population, not only in absolute numbers but also in numbers of households, can be more important.

Is the population composition transient? What are the ages, sex, incomes, occupations, education levels, family sizes, ethnic origins?

Who makes the purchasing decisions in the typical households and how frequently are purchases made? Are purchasers brand conscious or price conscious? Are they responsive to advertising?

Determine the purchasing power of the area. What is the average income and the disposable income? What are the lifestyles and trends of the present population and market?

Your local library, if you wish to do this type of useful research, can direct you to publications that provide census and other information.

You must use this census information intelligently and selectively. Decide exactly what you need that will be helpful to you and don't overwhelm yourself with useless data.

c. POTENTIAL SALES VOLUME

The main purpose of this market analysis is to establish your potential sales volume. This will become the forecast for your initial income statements.

One way to do this is to convert a percentage of your traffic count or trading area population into potential sales.

For example, if 1,000 pedestrians a day pass by your planned location, you might estimate that 5% of them could be purchasers (5% x 1,000 = 50 customers).

You might further estimate that average spending will be $10 per customer or 50 x $10 = $500 per day.

If you planned to be open 6 days a week, or let us say 300 days in a year, then total annual sales will be forecast at $500 x 300 = $150,000.

You can then use this information as the basis for preparing your financial plan, to be discussed in the next chapter.

d. SUMMARY

Some market research carried out in advance will at least show you that your business expectations were right. And if your product or service is not going to be successful, it is better to find this out before, rather than after the fact.

For example, if market research shows that your market is not nearly as large as you imagined, you might be able to scale down your plans until your market can be built up over time.

Well documented market research can also be invaluable in obtaining financing to help you open up your business. Without market analysis documentation, a potential lender is going to view your plans a lot less favorably.

9
FINANCIAL PLAN

In order to start and survive in business, you need a financial plan. You use a financial plan just like a map when traveling by car — it helps you get where you want to go.

A properly prepared plan will guide you in operating your business and help you to allocate your resources effectively and profitably. A sound financial plan will allow you to raise the necessary funds to operate your business successfully.

A combined market and financial plan (often referred to as a feasibility study by professionals who prepare them) is an in-depth analysis of the operational and financial feasibility of a new business, rather than an entrepreneur's guess that a new business will be economically viable.

A feasibility study, or plan, is not designed to prove that a new venture will be profitable. An independent plan professionally prepared by an impartial third party could result in either a positive or a negative recommendation.

If you prepare your own plan, you should take the same hard approach. If the forecast results are negative, both you and any potential lenders of funds for your new business should be happy that the idea goes no further.

However, if the forecast is positive, do not take it as a guarantee of success. A plan can only consider what is known at present and what may happen in the future. Since the future is impossible to forecast with absolute accuracy, and since so many unforeseeable factors can come into play, there are no guarantees. A plan may reduce, but does not eliminate, the risk of a new venture.

Your already completed market research results form the foundation of your financial plan.

a. FINANCIAL STATEMENTS

You may choose to put together your own financial plan. Alternatively, you may have your accountant do it. Even in the latter case, it will help if you know something about financial statements.

The two major statements in a set of financial statements are the balance sheet and the income statement. The balance sheet gives a picture of the financial position of a business at a particular point in time. The income statement shows the operating results of the business over a period of time. The period referred to on the income statement usually ends on the date of the balance sheet:

January 1		December 31
	Income	Balance
	Statement	Sheet

b. THE BALANCE SHEET

The balance sheet lists a business's assets or resources on the left-hand side. The right-hand, or credit, side lists liabilities (or debts of the company) and the shareholders' equity. On a balance sheet, total assets always equal total liabilities plus equity.

The asset side of the balance sheet is generally broken down into three sections:

(a) Current assets

(b) Fixed or long-term assets

(c) Other assets

1. Current assets

Current assets are cash or items that can or will be converted into cash within a short period of time (usually a year or less).

Current assets include items such as cash on hand, cash in the bank, accounts receivable, inventories, and prepaid expenses (insurance, property tax, and similar items that have been paid in advance but not "used up" at the balance sheet date).

2. Fixed or long-term assets

Fixed or long-term assets are relatively permanent, not intended for sale, and used in generating revenue.

Long-term assets include the land, building, fixtures, and equipment (including automotive equipment such as delivery trucks) that are owned by the business. These items are shown on the balance sheet at their cost.

Accumulated depreciation is deducted from the cost figures for building and equipment (but not land). Accumulated depreciation reflects the estimated decline in value of the assets due to wear and tear, the passage of time, changed economic conditions, or other factors.

The difference between the asset cost figure and the accumulated depreciation is referred to as net book value. Net book value does not necessarily accurately reflect the current market or replacement value of the assets.

3. Other assets

If a business has any other assets that do not fit into either the current or fixed categories they are included here. An example might be leasehold costs or improvements.

If improvements are made to a building that you are leasing, these improvements are of benefit during the life of the business or the remaining life of the lease. The costs should be spread over the life of the lease and so is much like depreciation, except that in cases such as leasehold property it is generally called amortization.

4. Total assets

The total of all the asset figures (current, fixed, and other) gives the total asset value, or total resources, of the business.

5. Liabilities and owners' equity

On the right-hand side of the balance sheet are the liabilities and owners' equity sections. The liabilities and equity side of the balance sheet shows how the assets have been financed, or paid for. The liability section comprises two categories: current liabilities and long-term liabilities.

Current liabilities are those debts that must be paid, or are expected to be paid, in less than a year.

Current liabilities include such items as accounts payable (for example, for purchases of inventory or supplies), accrued expenses (wages/salaries due to employees, payroll tax deductions, and similar items), income tax payable, and the portion of any long-term loans or mortgages that are due within the next year.

Long-term liabilities are the debts of the business that are payable more than one year after the balance sheet date. Included in this category would be mortgages and any similar long-term loans.

6. Owners' equity

In general terms, the owners' equity section of the balance sheet is the difference between the total assets and the total liabilities. It represents the equity, or the net worth, of the owners of the business. In an incorporated company, the owners' equity is made up of two main items: capital (shares) and retained earnings.

An incorporated company is limited by law to a maximum number of shares it can issue. This limit is known as the authorized number of shares. Shares generally have a par, or stated, value. It is this par value, multiplied by the number of shares actually issued (up to the authorized limit) that gives the total value of capital on the balance sheet.

The other part of the owners' equity section of the balance sheet is retained earnings. Retained earnings are the link between the income statement and the balance sheet. For that reason, retained earnings is discussed below, after you have had a chance to read about the income statement.

A typical balance sheet is illustrated in Sample #3.

c. THE INCOME STATEMENT

The income statement shows the operating results of the business for a period of time (month, quarter, half-year, or year). Formal income statements are prepared at least once a year (this is required when filing income tax returns, if for no other reason) and informal ones more frequently. The income statement shows income from sales (revenue) less any expenses made to achieve that revenue.

An income statement for a service firm (a travel agent) is illustrated in Sample #4.

However, in most types of retail firms, the income statement includes a cost of goods sold section that is deducted from revenue to produce a gross margin or gross profit figure before other expenses are deducted.

The reason for this is that the cost of goods sold figure and the gross profit to sales figure (expressed as a percentage of the related sales) are important benchmarks for measuring the success of the business. Sample #5 illustrates how cost of goods sold and gross profit are presented on an income statement.

The amount of detail concerning revenue and expenses to be shown on the income statement depends on the type and size of the business and the amount of information the owner/operator needs.

d. RETAINED EARNINGS

Usually the balance sheet and the income statement are accompanied by a statement of retained earnings. The statement of retained earnings is the place where the net profit of the business (from the income statement) for a period of time (let us say a year) is added to the preceding year's figure of retained earnings to give the new total.

In other words, the retained earnings are the accumulated net profits, less any losses, of the business since it began.

The retained earnings are not necessarily represented by cash in the bank because the money may have been used for other purposes, such as purchasing new equipment or expanding the size of the building.

A completed statement of retained earnings is illustrated in Sample #6. Note how the $66,000 of net profit from the income statement in Sample #5 has been transferred to the statement of retained earnings in Sample #6, and the year end retained earnings figure of $229,000 transferred to the balance sheet (Sample #3).

e. STATISTICAL INFORMATION

The first step in mapping out a financial plan for your new business is to obtain operating statistics for business similar to the one you propose starting so that you can forecast your first year's income statement.

It is preferable to obtain this information from similar types of businesses, but it is unlikely that you will get it from businesses with whom you are going to compete.

1. Key business ratios

A basic source of excellent information is a pamphlet put out annually by Dun and Bradstreet entitled Key Business Ratios. This publication lists various categories of retail businesses and their key operating ratios, such as cost of goods sold, gross profit or margin, net profit to sales, profit to net worth, sales to net worth, and sales to inventory, among others.

However, these are national average ratios and may not be typical of any one area

SAMPLE #3
BALANCE SHEET

RITA'S RETAIL LTD.   BALANCE SHEET   as at June 30, 19-

ASSETS				LIABILITIES & OWNERS' EQUITY			
Current Assets				**Current Liabilities**			
Cash		$ 8,000		Accounts payable		$ 9,000	
Accounts receivable		3,000		Accrued expenses		4,000	
Inventories		6,000		Income tax payable		3,000	
Prepaid expenses		5,000		Current portion of mortgage		17,000	
Total current assets		$ 22,000					
				Total current liabilities		$ 33,000	
Fixed Assets				**Long-Term Liabilities**			
Land, at cost		$ 72,000		Mortgage on building	140,000		
Building, at cost	$333,000			Less: current portion	17,000	123,000	
Less: Accumulated depreciation	57,000	276,000		**Total Liabilities**		$ 156,000	
Equipment, at cost	$ 74,000						
Less: Accumulated depreciation	45,000	29,000		**Owners' Equity**			
Total fixed assets		377,000		Capital — authorized 5,000			
				common shares @ $100 par value;			
Other Assets				issued and outstanding 200			
Deferred expense		6,000		shares	$ 20,000		
				Retained earnings	229,000	249,000	
Total Assets		$405,000		**Total Liabilities & Equity**		$405,000	

SAMPLE #4
INCOME STATEMENT — Service firm

SUNSATIONAL TRAVEL LTD.
Income Statement for Year Ending December 31, 199__

Operating revenues		$2,100,000
Payments to carriers and suppliers		1,900,000
Net commission income		$ 200,000
Operating expenses:		
Salaries and wages	$120,000	
Selling related costs	32,000	
Administration costs	22,000	
Rent and other	11,000	185,000
Profit before tax		$ 15,000
Income tax		6,000
Net profit		$ 9,000

RITA'S RETAIL LTD.
INCOME STATEMENT
For Year Ending June 30, 199__

Sales	$1,250,000
Cost of goods sold	750,000
Gross profit	$ 500,000
Operating expenses:	
(listed in detail)	368,000
Profit before income tax	$ 132,000
Income tax	66,000
Net profit	$ 66,000

RITA'S RETAIL LTD.
STATEMENT OF RETAINED EARNINGS
For Year Ending June 30 199__

Retained earnings beginning of year	$193,000
Add profit for year	66,000
	$259,000
Deduct dividends paid	30,000
Retained earnings June 30, 199__	$229,000

or business in that area. You need to try to search out information for your local area from sources such as:

(a) Local Chamber of Commerce or Board of Trade

(b) Government departments for small business

(c) Financial institutions such as banks

(d) Financial newspapers and magazines

(e) Sales and marketing management magazines

(f) Business, trade, and professional associations

(g) Market research and advertising companies

(h) Local university and college departments teaching business administration

2. Preparing an income statement

From the statistical information obtained in your market research concerning potential annual sales you should be able to build an income statement. For example, you can apply the cost of goods sold percent figure to the calculated potential sales to arrive at gross profit or margin.

From this you can deduct other operating expenses, including a reasonable salary for yourself, applying appropriate expense to sales figures for each separate expense to arrive at a net income to sales figure.

The net income arrived at should be sufficient to give you a reasonable return on the investment. This return should be at least 10%, otherwise you might be better to leave your investment funds in the bank and eliminate the risk of trying to run your own business.

f. INVESTMENT REQUIRED

In order to see if the net profit is going to provide the suggested minimum 10% return, you must also determine what kind of total investment in the business is required.

Your investment costs might include the purchase of land at the location you want. This will be a known and fairly specific cost. You may also need to purchase the building in which you are going to operate. Again, this will be a fairly specific and exact cost. In other cases, you may be constructing a building, in which case construction costs can be estimated using the approach suggested earlier and in Sample #1.

Even in rented premises you will have start-up costs for improvements to the premises such as painting and decorating, walls or partitions, and plumbing or electrical changes.

You will also probably need fixtures (such as lighting, counters, shelving, and indoor and outdoor signs) as well as certain types of equipment such as sales registers.

All of these costs should be estimated. Sample #7 may help you summarize these costs.

1. Pre-opening and operating costs

In addition, you will also have to estimate your pre-opening costs. These are the costs that you incur prior to opening your doors and making sales to provide cash flow.

You also need to forecast the operating costs for the first two or three months to make sure you have enough opening cash to pay these expenses until cash starts flowing into the business.

Sample #8 may help you summarize your pre-opening and operating costs. Note that on this sample you should add 10% to the total of these costs for contingencies. It is easy to overestimate sales and underestimate costs, and the contingency may help compensate for this.

g. FINANCIAL ANALYSIS

In a formal feasibility study you might need much more detail than has been suggested so far. In fact, the financial analysis section of

SAMPLE #7
FIXTURES AND EQUIPMENT WORKSHEET

Item	Estimated cost
Counters	$
Display stands	
Shelving	
Cabinets	
Tables	
Window display fixtures	
Lighting	
Cash register	
Safe	
Office equipment	
Delivery equipment	
Outdoor sign	
Decorating/remodeling	
TOTAL — Enter on Pre-opening Worksheet (see Sample #8)	

SAMPLE #8
WORKSHEET FOR PRE-OPENING AND OPERATING EXPENSES

ESTIMATED MONTHLY OPERATING COSTS

Item

Owner/manager salary $_____

Other employee salary/wages   _____

Advertising   _____

Delivery   _____

Insurance   _____

Interest   _____

Legal and accounting   _____

License   _____

Maintenance   _____

Supplies   _____

Telephone   _____

Utilities   _____

Other   _____

Total of above $_____

Multiply this total by 3 $_____

Pre-opening Costs $_____

Starting inventory   _____

Advertising   _____

Legal and accounting   _____

License   _____

Utility deposit   _____

Cash on hand   _____

Other   _____

Total of Operating and Pre-opening Costs $_____

Add 10% for contingency   _____

Fixtures and equipment total (from Sample #7) $_____

Total estimated investment required $_____

a feasibility study is usually broken down into the following subsections:

(a) Capital investment required and tentative financing plan

(b) Projected income statements for at least the first year and for as far ahead as five years

(c) Projected cash flow statement for at least the first year and for as far ahead as five years

(d) An evaluation of the financial projections and the economic viability of the new retail store

Preparing the financial analysis can be a fairly complex matter that requires the expertise of someone with an accounting background. Unless your situation is fairly simple, use a professional consultant or accountant. Also, lenders are more likely to be convinced to part with money if the feasibility study is professionally prepared.

Finally, if the financial projections appear to be negative it is better that you know this now rather than two or three years down the road when your business is bankrupt.

Despite all these cautions, you may still decide to prepare your own feasibility study. In that case you might wish to refer to professional guide manuals that are available for both new retail and new service ventures that will take you through the necessary steps of a business plan feasibility study.

In the U.S., write to:

U.S. Small Business Administration
P.O. Box 15434
Fort Worth, TX 76119

and ask for MA 2.020 *Business Plan for Retailers* and/or MA 2.026 *Feasibility Checklist for Starting a Small Business.*

In Canada, contact your local branch of the FBDB and ask for their current brochure on do-it-yourself kits.

Federal Business Development Bank
800 Victoria Square
Tour de la Place - Victoria
P.O. Box 335
Montreal, PQ
H4Z 1L4

10
EQUITY VERSUS DEBT FINANCING

Now that you know from your financial plan what total initial investment is required, and that you should obtain a reasonable return on this investment, you can begin deciding how this investment will be financed. In general, there are two main sources of funding any business: debt and equity.

With debt the lender does not have any equity or ownership in the business and thus normally no active say in the day-to-day operations of the business. Banks are one type of debt lender. Their return on the investment (loan) made is the interest the borrower pays on the use of that money.

However, before you can raise any debt financing, you normally have to show potential lenders that you are willing to invest (and risk) money in the business yourself. If you are not willing to invest in the business yourself by way of equity, then why should an outside lender by way of debt?

a. EQUITY FINANCING

This equity investment could range from 10% to 50% of the total investment. The closer to 50% it is, the easier it will be to borrow and the higher your profits might be (since you will have less interest expense on borrowed money that will eat into those profits).

1. Personal funds

The most common source of equity capital is personal funds from savings. Over the past few years many retail entrepreneurs have been able to provide this initial equity because of inflation that caused their home ownership values to increase to the point

that the home could be remortgaged to provide a form of instant cash.

2. Friends or relatives

This equity could be further increased from the savings of friends willing to invest, or even from relatives ("love money"). However, many otherwise successful small businesses have created problems by bringing in friends and/or relatives as investors.

Mixing social or family relationships with business is always risky, particularly if the business is not doing as well as everyone initially imagined, or if the terms and conditions of such loans are not clearly spelled out to prevent these lenders insisting on becoming involved in day-to-day operational matters. Also, if a relative dies, the heirs may immediately demand their money back, with interest, under the threat of a lawsuit.

To avoid these problems, make sure any friend or family loans are covered by written agreements, preferably drawn up by a lawyer. In this way, agreements will be viewed as businesslike by the lenders.

Agreement should be reached on such matters as rate of interest to be paid, when the loans will be retired (paid back), and any option you have to pay them back early. Also covered should be the procedures that all parties follow if loans become delinquent.

3. Shares

Unless your company is a proprietorship or partnership, it will have to issue some shares. In a one-person company, those shares are held by the owner. A larger company may possibly have several owners or shareholders, some of whom could be friends or relatives who want to invest in your new business by purchasing shares rather than by offering direct loans.

4. Loans versus shares

The total "equity" investment (i.e., the money you can raise by not going to outside lenders such as banks) could be in the form of loans, or common stock or shares in the company if it is incorporated, or a combination of loans and shares. How the owners' or equity investors' investment in the company is structured will vary in each situation.

However, generally speaking, the advantage of the money being invested by way of loans is that it can more easily be paid back to lenders without tax, other than personal tax on any interest received from the company before all the loan is finally paid off.

If the money is in the form of shares, the lenders will find it much more difficult to withdraw since shares must be sold to someone else, or be repurchased by the company, and may be subject to personal capital gains tax.

On the other hand, equity investor loans, because of the ease with which they can be repaid, are looked upon with skepticism by banks and other debt investors since it would be feasible for the business to borrow money from a debt lender and use the cash to pay back equity investor loans.

The long-term debt investors may therefore place restrictions or conditions on when and how the company can pay off shareholder loans, redeem shares, or possibly even pay dividends on shares. These restrictions or conditions are imposed to protect the long-term debt investors.

In particular, the advice of tax accountants is suggested since your personal tax situation, and that of any other equity investors, and the degree of financial success

of the business can have a bearing on whether the shareholder's investment should be in the form of loans or purchase of shares.

b. DEBT FINANCING

The other type of financing available to a business is debt. An important aspect of debt is the interest rate you will have to pay on this borrowed money.

1. Interest

Banks and other financial institutions vary interest rates according to money market conditions. The rates can change frequently. They also vary depending on the customer. The prime rate is generally the lowest rate available. Rates increase above that depending on the specific business, its credit rating, its size, and other factors.

It would not be unreasonable (because of the risk involved to the lender) to suggest that most small retail businesses in need of bank credit pay rates that are among the highest.

Lenders who have pools of funds available from depositors who have left money with them for a minimum of at least a year, and preferably longer, may be able to lend money at lower rates than those charged on short-term loans.

However, in volatile money markets where interest rates and the money market are unpredictable, it sometimes happens that long-term lending rates, since they are fixed and not subject to change during the term of the loan, are higher than current short-term rates.

Because of this, and the fact that lenders have been hurt in volatile money markets, it is often the case nowadays that you will be unable to obtain a fixed interest rate on a long-term loan.

2. Balloon payments

These long-term loans may also be subject to two- or three-year terms and balloon payments. A balloon payment simply means that at the end of the two- or three-year term the lender calls in the loan and you must negotiate, usually on the lender's terms, a new loan for the amount still owing on the old one.

3. Variable rate

Even variable rate long-term loans are now more common. A variable rate loan simply means that the interest rates are adjustable by the lender, as frequently as monthly, either up or down depending on money market conditions. These market conditions can take into consideration the current inflation rate and the market's expectation of the future inflation rate.

4. Lender competition

Since banks are in competition with other banks or other financial lending institutions, these interest rates are competitive, just as your prices have to be.

Therefore, in seeking a loan you should search out the lender with the most favorable lending rate and conditions, just as you would expect astute customers to seek you out if you offered the best quality at a competitive price.

5. Security

Another important aspect of borrowing money by debt is security.

Most lenders require some sort of security for loans made to small businesses. For intermediate- and long-term loans this security is quite specific and is discussed in a later chapter. For short-term loans of a year or less, this security is probably a personal guarantee.

6. Personal guarantees

Even if your business is incorporated, the lender may require this guarantee or endorsement of the loan in case your company does not meet its debt obligations. This means that if your company defaults on its repayments, the lender can claim against your personal assets such as your savings, your home, your car, or other personal assets.

Normally, particularly if your case for a loan is not a strong one, you will have little choice but to provide this personal guarantee or endorsement. If there are other shareholders in the company, they might also be required to sign guarantees.

In some cases, when neither you nor other principals in the company can provide sufficient security to the lender, you may be asked to find an outside guarantor. If your case is so weak that you need an outside guarantor, you might question whether or not you should really be making the loan.

This guarantee may be limited or unlimited. A limited guarantee gives the lender the right to demand that you repay, on request, the amount owing on a specific loan. An unlimited guarantee gives the lender the right to demand that you repay, on request, all loans due to that lender. Obviously, it is preferable for you to have a limited guarantee.

Make sure that when any guaranteed loan is paid off, you obtain a release from the guarantee. If a personal guarantee is required by the lender in addition to other security, try to negotiate a guarantee only for the amount of the shortfall and not for the full amount of the loan.

Also, if you or any other equity investors have made a direct loan to the company and were obliged by the debt lender to sign a postponement of claim for your own loan, make sure that the postponement of claim is also canceled.

Similarly, if during the period of the debt, restrictions were placed on payment of dividends to you, or if life insurance policies were assigned to the lender, have these restrictions removed and/or the policies changed.

c. OTHER ALTERNATIVES

You may be able to obtain a loan, all else failing, by assigning your savings account to the lender as security. While it is assigned, your withdrawals from it will be limited.

Another alternative is to raise cash from your life insurance policy. However, instead of raising cash from your insurance company based on your policy's paid up cash value, you may be able to raise the cash by assigning it instead to a bank since it may be easier and speedier to obtain the cash that way.

Finally, if you have marketable stocks and bonds, you may be able to use them as security or collateral for a loan. These would have to be gilt-edged stocks, and the maximum you could expect might be up to 75% of their market value. Alternatively, if you had government bonds, you might get 90%. If the market value on your stocks and bonds drops while they are secured, you may at that time have to put up additional collateral or reduce the loan.

11
SHORT-TERM FINANCING

In most retail businesses that are being started, the greatest need is for short-term financing.

Short-term financing generally is funding required for a period of less than one year. In short-term financing the lender tends to place greater emphasis on your balance sheet in order to see if, in case of your business's liquidation, current assets would provide sufficient funds to repay the debt.

This differs from intermediate- and long-term financing (discussed in the next chapter) where lenders rely more on the earning power of your company and its ability to repay longer loans out of ongoing profits.

One basic rule of finance is that short-term requirements for cash should be provided by short-term financing, and longer-term requirements by intermediate- or long-term financing.

If this rule is not followed, you might end up with a financing imbalance. This could happen, for example, if you made a one-year bank loan and used this money to buy long-term equipment. You might then find yourself short of cash to purchase inventory, carry receivables, pay your payables, and even short of cash to pay back the one-year loan! You could even be forced into liquidation or bankruptcy in such a situation.

Some of the various methods of short-term financing are as follows.

a. TRADE CREDIT

Surprisingly, the most common means of short-term financing is trade credit or financial assistance from other companies with which you do business. The reason for this is that most suppliers do not demand cash on delivery other than in those cases where a business has a reputation for delinquency in payment of accounts.

Usually a bill or invoice for purchases is sent at the month end. For example, in the case of a 30-day payment period for items purchased at the beginning of a month, you use the service or supplies received without cost for anywhere up to 60 days.

To a retail business, this type of trade credit is an important source of cash. Even if you had the cash to pay the bill at the time it was received, it may not be wise to do so.

As long as there is no penalty imposed, you are free to let your cash sit in the bank and collect interest until the invoice has to be paid. To you this is another source of profit.

1. Open credit

This type of trade credit is sometimes called "open credit" since it is generally arranged on an understanding between buyer and seller without any formal agreement documented in writing, and is useful in financing the inventory of a new business.

For example, if you purchase $25,000 of inventory you might put up $10,000 cash and owe the suppliers the balance to be paid 30 days later. During that 30 days most, if not all, of that inventory will be sold at a profit and you will have the cash to pay off the $15,000 owed. This cycle can be repeated indefinitely.

There are three typical methods of arranging payment with a supplier: cash on delivery (COD), no cash discount, and cash discount.

The first arrangement, COD, in effect means that the purchaser does not receive any trade credit. Cash must be paid at the time of delivery.

The second, more common, arrangement is for the supplier to extend credit for a specific number of days after delivery of the goods, or after the month end following delivery of the goods, with no cash discount permitted. In other words, the full amount of all invoices must be paid.

The third arrangement is for the supplier to offer both a credit period and a cash discount. One common type is referred to as 2/10, net 30. This means that you are offered a 2% discount off the invoice price if the bill is paid within 10 days. If the bill is not paid within the 10-day period, it must be paid within a further 30 days but without discount. This type of arrangement is made to encourage you to pay bills promptly.

With a 2/10, net 30 arrangement, you must seriously consider the cost of not taking the discount. For example, if you make a $1,000 purchase and pay within 10 days, the amount to be paid is $980. If the discount is not taken, in effect, you have the use of the $980 for a further 20 days. However, the cost of this would be:

$$\frac{\$20}{\$980} \quad X \quad \frac{365}{20} = 37.2\%$$

This is a very expensive form of financing. Even if you are short of cash, it might be wise to borrow $980 from the bank to pay within the discount period, since the bank interest expense would probably be considerably less than 37%.

While a bank loan might accomplish the same end as using trade credit, you might find it difficult to obtain that bank loan as a new company. You might also find the burden of the interest plus principal repayments difficult to carry.

By paying cash on delivery for initial orders from suppliers to establish and maintain good supplier relations you can build up a solid credit base with a supplier.

You should also be ready to provide a supplier with credit references. Most larger suppliers have credit departments or employ an agency to check on your credit status if you are a new customer desiring trade credit.

Having established a good credit standing with a supplier, pay your bills on time; otherwise, you might find yourself being reverted to a COD basis. Maintaining a good credit record with a supplier may mean that one day your supplier will be interested in investing money in your business for purposes of expansion.

Also, as you build up your credit record with suppliers, you might later be able to negotiate more favorable trade credit terms, such as extending the time period before payment is required, or getting a larger discount on invoices paid promptly.

However, don't become too attached to one or two suppliers simply because they provide liberal trade credit terms. You might find you are locked into a situation when a supplier's prices no longer remain competitive in terms of price, quality, delivery, or service.

Also advise suppliers, particularly major ones, in advance if you have to defer payment of their account for some reason. Alerting suppliers might prevent ill will and credit curtailment if, for example, your business is suffering a slight downturn in difficult economic times.

Don't forget that in difficult economic conditions the supplier might also be forced to curtail trade credit. In other words, trade credit is not a right that you have in perpetuity.

2. Stretching payables

In the discussion so far, it is assumed that you pay bills before the end of the supplier's payment period. If you delay paying beyond that date, you are using this "free" money at a further cost to the supplier.

For this reason, suppliers do not encourage the practice. Banks and other lending institutions also look unfavorably on businesses that make a habit of not paying bills promptly.

If you have this reputation, you might well find that suppliers will deliver only on a COD basis. You might also find it difficult to borrow short-term funds when you need them.

However, if the nature of your business is seasonal, you might find it difficult to pay all bills in the off-season when they are due. In such cases, it might be wise to pre-arrange for a longer payment period with suppliers whose financial resources allow them to extend longer credit.

Alternatively, arrangements could be made with a lending institution to borrow funds for the interim period so that bills can be paid within the normal payment period.

You should also recognize that trade credit is not absolutely "free." The supplier who extends credit also has financing costs which must be paid out of revenue from the products sold. In other words, the cost is included in the selling prices. Where competition exists among suppliers, however, this hidden cost should be minimized.

3. Goods on consignment

Another type of trade credit is to obtain goods on consignment. This is common in certain types of business. When you receive goods on consignment, the supplier retains ownership of them. You pay only when the goods are sold.

b. SHORT-TERM OR OPERATING LOANS

Short-term or operating loans are for financing inventory, accounts receivable, special purchases, prepaid promotions, and other items requiring working capital during peak periods. Normally up to 10% of annual sales can be borrowed to finance such requirements.

Short-term loans are sometimes referred to as commercial loans. They are considered to be self-liquidation loans since they are paid back when the inventory or receivables financed by them are converted to cash that is used to pay off the loan.

The main sources of short-term loans are commercial banks or similar financial institutions. Using a short-term loan is a good way to establish credit with a bank. When such a lender considers a short-term loan it is very interested in your business's liquidity. If you have a healthy working capital, collect your accounts receivable promptly, and have a rapid rate of inventory turnover, your business is a good prospect for a short-term loan.

1. Security required

This type of loan could be secured or unsecured. If secured, the security might be any or all of the following:

(a) A fixed or floating charge debenture on accounts receivable, inventory, equipment, or fixtures. The lender can register this debenture in a similar way to a mortgage on land and building.

(b) A general assignment of your accounts receivable. You collect the receivable in the normal way unless you are in default of the loan. In that case, the lender assumes collection of the receivables. When receivables are assigned you normally have to submit a list of those outstanding each month to the lender.

(c) An assignment of fire insurance and, in some cases, key employee or personal life insurance policies

(d) Stocks or bonds that you or your company owns

(e) A personal guarantee by you and/or your spouse (when personal assets are registered in the spouse's name)

Short-term loans are usually negotiated for specific periods of time (for example 30, 60, or 90 days and, less frequently, for periods up to a year or more) and may be repayable in a lump sum at the end of the period, or in periodic installments (e.g., monthly).

If you have adequate collateral, short-term loans of up to a year can sometimes be negotiated.

Each loan is usually covered by a promissory note (a form of contract spelling out the interest rate and terms of the loan). The interest rate is frequently subject to change, particularly in erratic money markets.

2. Discounting

Discounting means that the interest on the loan is deducted in advance. The interest rate on term loans is usually a stated annual interest rate. The rate may differ from the effective (or true) rate if the loan is discounted.

If a $1,000 bank loan is taken out at the beginning of the year to be repaid at the end of the year at a discount (interest) rate of 15%, you would receive $850 ($1,000, less 15% of $1,000, or $150), and repay $1,000 at the end of the year. Since you have only $850, the effective interest rate is:

$$\frac{\$150}{\$850} \times 100 = 17.6\%$$

The effective interest rate also differs from the stated rate if a loan is repayable in equal installments over the term of the loan, rather than in a lump sum at the end of the loan period as was the case above.

Consider a $1,200 loan at a 12% rate, repayable in equal monthly installments of

principal over a year ($100 per month) plus interest. If the interest is calculated on the initial loan, it will be 12% of $1,200, or $144 ($12 per month).

The effective rate of interest will be higher than the stated 12%, however, since you do not have the use of the full $1,200 for the year.

There are tables (available at most bookstores) with which you can figure out an exact rate of interest under various circumstances, but you can quickly calculate an approximate effective rate of interest yourself.

With equal monthly repayments, on average the borrower has only half the $1,200 to use over the year, or $600 ($1,200 divided by 2). The effective interest rate is then:

$$\frac{\$144}{\$600} \times 100 = 24$$

This is double the stated rate.

In all cases where money is borrowed, and particularly if you are shopping around for the best rate, it is important to know what the effective interest rate is.

c. LINE OF CREDIT

A line of credit is an agreement between you and a bank, or similar financial institution, specifying the maximum amount of credit (overdraft) the bank will allow you at any one time.

Credit lines are usually established for one-year periods, subject to annual renegotiation and renewal, with the bank taking your accounts receivable and inventory as security.

Generally, accounts receivable, as long as they are not overdue, may be financed up to 75% and inventory up to 50%.

The amount of credit is based on the bank's assessment of the creditworthiness of your business and its credit requirements. This type of loan is sometimes called a demand loan since the bank can demand that it be repaid immediately without notice. However, this would not happen under normal circumstances.

A business with a line of credit of any sizable amount (usually $100,000 or more) is generally required to keep a deposit balance with the lender. This deposit balance is usually proportional to the amount of the line of credit. For example, it might be stipulated by the lender at 10% to 15% of the line of credit amount. This percentage might vary with the money market.

Since the deposit amount is generally in an account that pays little or no interest, it favors the bank and increases the effective interest rate you are paying on any money used from your line of credit. Some banks accept fees or a higher interest rate in lieu of a compensating balance.

In order to secure a line of credit you may have to sign short-term notes to evidence the advances. These notes are periodically reviewed and repaid, reduced, or extended, as required. If you must clear up the credit line annually, you may have to borrow from another source or take cash from some other source. This may mean you will not be able to pay bonuses or dividends that you had otherwise planned to pay.

Establishing of a line of credit protects you since normally lenders do not reduce or cancel the line of credit without good cause. However, the lender keeps an eye on your financial statements and economic and other factors that might influence your business's operations and change the lender's view of the appropriateness of your line of credit.

A line of credit is useful for a seasonal business with an inventory turnover that creates a peak seasonal financial need. In such a situation a line of credit is the usual answer to cash needs.

With a line of credit you pay interest only on money actually borrowed — not on the full amount of the line of credit. This interest may be supplemented by a small commitment fee of less than 1% on any unused portion of the line of credit.

d. OTHER LOANS

Some other types of loans are as follows.

1. Collateral loan

You may be able to obtain a bank loan on the basis of collateral such as a chattel mortgage, stocks and bonds, cash surrender value of life insurance, and similar security.

Even with this collateral, regardless of how good it is, the lender may feel that it is no guarantee of your business's ability to repay since the lender's objective is not to cash in the collateral since it may produce less in liquidation than the amount you owe.

However, the collateral does afford the lender some security and a collateral loan may be easier to find than a line of credit or unsecured loan for a risky business.

2. Character loan

A character loan is a short-term unsecured loan, generally restricted to an individual or his or her company with an excellent credit rating.

3. Floor planning

Floor planning is used as a financing vehicle by retailers of large ticket items (automobiles, appliances) that can be readily identified, usually by a serial number, and that have a relatively high unit value.

In floor planning, you have possession of the units and the lender retains the ownership and pays the manufacturer the cost price of the items. As you sell each item you pay the lender the amount due on that item.

You generally sign a note to the lender and pay interest from the time the arrangement is made until the time the item is sold. A flooring line might be renewed annually.

4. Indirect collection financing

Indirect collection financing is also used for big ticket items on an installment basis. The lender advances 70% to 80% of the value of each item as it is sold. The retailer repays the advance with interest as the consumer/purchaser pays each installment.

5. Chattel mortgage

A chattel mortgage loan is usually for a short- or intermediate-term situation. It is secured by the movable assets (chattels) of your business that are not otherwise mortgaged or secured. The chattel mortgage provides a lien to the lender.

To obtain the mortgage for your business, you might have to include personal assets in the security.

The value assigned to the assets is their current liquidation value. You may be required to carry various types of insurance on the mortgaged chattels.

The security is released or discharged to you when the loan is repaid.

6. Floating charge debenture

A floating charge debenture is again a short- or intermediate-term loan situation where the loan is secured by a general claim on the total equity of the business.

A floating charge debenture does not describe specific assets as security (unlike a chattel mortgage or a commercial pledge). Instead, all the assets are described in general terms and can be disposed of in the ordinary day-to-day operations of the business unless you default on the loan.

As a precaution, the lender may impose certain restrictions or controls to ensure that your business's equity does not fall below what the lender deems is required to secure the loan.

A business with a floating charge debenture may still be able to obtain other short-term financing on specific assets through, for example, a chattel mortgage.

12
INTERMEDIATE- AND LONG-TERM FINANCING

Most financing that is not short-term, in other words that is for more than one year, is often referred to as long-term. However, somewhere between short- and long-term financing is intermediate-term financing for items not generally purchased on a regular basis, such as equipment and fixtures for your new business.

a. INTERMEDIATE-TERM FINANCING

When considering an intermediate-term loan, lending companies rely on indications of your business's profitability and ability to repay. These indications are provided by income statement and cash flow forecasts for the next several years, as long as these forecasts are reasonable and not made on the basis of overestimated sales and underestimated expenses.

1. Term loans

A common way to obtain intermediate-term financing is through term loans. Term loans are usually obtained from banks or similar financial institutions, but, unlike short-term loans, are usually arranged to cover the purchase of basic inventory, leasehold improvements, and assets such as furniture, fixtures, and equipment. Generally 60% to 75% of the cost of these items can be obtained through term loans.

Term loans are usually repaid in regular installments of principal and interest over the life of the loan, which is usually less than the life of the assets for which financing is

required. Term loans could vary in length from one to five years.

The interest rate on term loans is usually a percentage point or more higher than that for a short-term loan made to the same borrower.

The periodic payments on term loans can be geared to the business's cash flow ability to repay. In some cases, only the interest portion of such loans is payable in the first year or two. Payments could be monthly, quarterly, semi-annually, or annually. Payments are calculated so that the debt is repaid (amortized) by a specific date.

If the periodic payments do not completely amortize the debt by the maturity date, the final payment will be larger than the previous periodic payments. This larger, final payment is known as a "balloon" payment. Term loans sometimes allow early repayment without penalty.

Interest rates may also be negotiable. As long as you adhere to the terms of the loan, you can generally be assured that no payments other than regular installments will be required before the due date of the loan.

Term loans have an advantage in that they develop a lender/borrower relationship over a number of years that can be useful in future financial matters, including advice from the lender concerning preferable future financing arrangements that you could make.

Sometimes personal term loans are available to help finance your initial equity investment in the business. However, this can be risky since the total interest cost on all loans (since none of the money is your own) can be crippling to the company's working capital.

The term loan usually requires a written loan agreement that, among other things, might limit your company's ability to incur other debts, owner salaries, and dividend payments. In addition, the agreement may require that a stipulated percentage of company profits be used to increase repayment installments on the loan or the loan may be considered in default. Compensating balances are also frequently required.

Most term loans are only offered to companies with profit histories whose current or projected financial statements demonstrate an ability to repay. For that reason, a term loan may not be easy to find for a new retail business.

2. Installment financing

As an alternative, installment financing could be used to finance the purchase of equipment of various kinds, including automotive equipment, and fixtures (such as counters, shelves, and display cases) where term loans are unavailable.

By using an equipment loan, you can retain precious working capital. Lenders generally finance from 60% to 80% of the asset's value. The balance is your down payment.

Although some furniture and equipment sales companies may finance this way directly, others sell to a financing company that, in turn, does the installment financing.

Many supply companies act as an intermediary between you and the finance company to coordinate the arrangement. In other cases, you may have to shop around to arrange your own installment financing.

Since the assets being financed generally have a life averaging 5 to 10 years, the financing agency runs a relatively high risk because of the very low value of second-hand fixtures and equipment (and thus its low value as collateral). So the lifespan of such financing is usually from 3 to 7 years. Repayments of principal and interest are monthly, and the interest rate is generally much higher than with term loans — it could run as much as five or six points over prime.

Installment loans are generally secured by a chattel mortgage (a lien on the assets financed), which can be registered and which permits the seller or lending company to sell the liened assets if the installment payments are in default.

Alternatively, the lender's security could be a conditional sales contract, which gives the lender title to the assets until you have satisfied all the terms of the contract.

The installment loan agreement usually binds you to maintaining working capital at an agreed upon level and to obtain lender approval before making any capital expenditure over a specified limit. It might also limit the amount that can be paid in salaries and bonuses, and require that assets be kept free of encumbrances.

Finally, the agreement might require that a proportion of profits be applied to loan repayments above and beyond the amount stipulated in your note payable securing the installment loan.

b. LONG-TERM FINANCING

Where long-term debt is required (for example, to purchase land or to build or purchase a building), it will probably be in the form of a mortgage.

A mortgage is a grant by the borrower to a creditor or lender, of preference or priority in a particular asset. This asset is usually some type of real estate.

If the borrower is in default (for example, for nonpayment of interest or principal), the creditor holding the mortgage is entitled to force the sale of the specific asset pledged as security. Proceeds of the sale go to the holder of the first mortgage before any other creditors receive anything.

If another creditor had a mortgage on the same asset, he or she is classified as a second mortgage holder, and ranks below the first mortgage holder but above a third mortgage holder (if one exists) or other creditors of the borrower in default.

The legal procedure by which the first mortgage holder can force the sale is called foreclosure.

First mortgage lenders are generally organizations that have collected savings from many individual investors or lenders. The organization, acting as an intermediary, centralizes these savings and lends them in lump sums.

Such organizations are insurance companies, pension companies, real estate investment trusts, commercial and mortgage banks, and even trust companies and credit unions.

1. Feasibility studies and other requirements

Before lending money, these organizations consider factors such as your track record. If you have a proven record of five years or more of successful experience in business, you are more likely to obtain funds at a reasonable rate than a novice.

Lenders are also concerned about the amount of equity invested by the owner. This equity usually takes the form of a direct cash investment in shares if the company is incorporated. Without such equity investment, the mortgage lender is taking a very high-risk position.

Generally, such equity needs to be a minimum of 25% to 30% of total required financing. In other words, if the total investment cost were $100,000 you would need $25,000 to $30,000 of personal cash invested.

A prospective lender is also concerned that proper accounting procedures, particularly for cost control, are instituted. Lenders frequently require audited financial statements at least yearly but sometimes more frequently. This allows them to read possible danger signs before it is too late.

Some lenders carry out on-site inspections of properties in which they have investments to ensure that the property is not run-down and that it is maintained adequately. This ensures that their investment is better protected. In some cases, the mortgage investor stipulates that a percentage of annual revenue be spent on property maintenance.

2. Loan terms

Generally, first mortgages can be obtained for up to 70% or 75% of the appraised value of the land and/or building offered as security for the loan. If the land is leased, then the mortgage is usually obtainable only on the appraised value of the building.

Loan terms usually range up to a maximum of 20 to 25 years. However, the term could be as short as 10 years.

Repayment of loans is generally made in equal monthly payments of principal and interest. These payments are calculated so that, at the stated interest rate, the regular payments will completely amortize (pay off) the mortgage by the end of its life.

Sometimes the payments are calculated so that, during the early years, interest only is paid (with no reduction in principal).

3. Early payment

Most first mortgage loans do not permit any early payment for at least the first several years. Thus, you are locked in for that period and cannot benefit if interest rates decline.

Where prepayment is permitted, the mortgagor may impose a penalty. The penalty is usually a percentage of the balance still owing, and the percentage may decline as time goes by. It may be to your benefit to pay such a penalty.

For example, if the initial mortgage carried an 18% interest rate, and current rates had declined to 14%, you might be able to negotiate a new loan with a new lender, and use part of the proceeds to pay off the remaining balance of the initial mortgage plus penalty. The penalty imposition may be more than offset by the interest reduction over the term of the new mortgage.

Since circumstances in each case differ, each decision about long-term mortgage refinancing must be made on its own merits.

4. Call provision

Just as you may be permitted early payment opportunities to benefit from changed general market interest rates, so too is the lender usually protected. Most mortgage agreements have a call provision in them.

A call provision allows the lender, after a stated number of years, to ask for complete repayment of the mortgage. The lender and borrower then renegotiate a new interest rate for a further stipulated period of time. A lender would probably call a loan if interest rates had increased since the original mortgage agreement was signed.

There is also an increasing trend toward variable interest rate mortgages where the interest rate, depending on market conditions, can be changed up or down by the lender as frequently as monthly.

5. Other compensation

Some lenders require additional compensation such as a fee, discount, or bonus. For example, a $10,000 bonus on a $250,000 mortgage would mean you receive only $240,000 but must pay back principal and interest on the $250,000. Such front-end "loads" obviously raise the effective interest rate.

Other lenders may ask for an equity participation. Equity participation increases the lender's return on investment while diluting yours. Equity might take the form of a percentage of annual revenue, or an investment in common shares.

6. Joint venture

In some cases, the lender might enter into a joint venture agreement with you. Such an agreement might provide you with some equity funds (while giving up part of equity control), as well as mortgage funds.

In other cases, the mortgage investor might supply 100% of the total project cost for which he or she receives a substantial equity position. This might significantly reduce your capital outlay, and at the same time reduce your risk, control, and potential future income.

7. Equipment and fixtures

Most long-term mortgage lenders do not normally finance any portion of your equipment and fixtures. The prime reason is that mortgage lenders are in the long-term loan business, and furniture and equipment have a relatively short-term life.

However, despite this, they sometimes attempt to obtain a first mortgage on these chattels (in addition to the long-term mortgage on the assets that they have financed).

In this way, if the first mortgage lender has to foreclose, he or she is sure that the equipment and fixtures will not be removed and that the business can continue to operate.

8. Second mortgages

Second mortgages are also used for financing land and building. A second mortgage lender takes a second lien on the property mortgaged. The loan amount is generally limited to 5% to 15% of the appraised value of the property, and loan terms usually range from 5 to 15 years.

Second mortgage interest rates are generally three to four points above first mortgage rates because of the additional risk involved. Repayments are made by you over the life of the loan in equal monthly installments of principal and interest.

An excessive second mortgage can be risky to both you and the lender because of potential cash flow problems if the business is not successful.

13
BORROWING MONEY

The amount of financing required to start up your new retail business depends on the type of business, whether premises can be rented or must be built or purchased, the amount of start-up inventory that must be purchased, and the amount of working capital required until cash can be generated from sales.

A service business (e.g., barber shop, real estate, employment agency) may require little or no initial investment and, in some cases, can be operated out of a home.

If the business can be started with little or no borrowed money, when it proves successful, financing from outside sources will be easier.

a. INVESTMENT PROJECTIONS

A new business has to be fairly precise in its projections of investment required, as well as forecasts of revenue and expenses over the initial months, and possibly even years, to indicate if the business will be profitable. This is why you need a market and financial plan, as discussed earlier.

Cash flow calculations must be part of the overall projections since that will show, among other things, whether or not cash will be generated to repay any loans made to start up the business.

The larger the business, and the more that has to be borrowed, the more detailed your financial plan has to be since lenders are not sympathetic to requests for funding supported by figures scratched out on the back of an envelope.

b. WHAT'S INVOLVED IN SEEKING FINANCING?

Knowing what's involved in securing financing can give you a distinct advantage. The most important fact to remember is that you are in competition with other people and other businesses for the same money.

It is often said that there is a shortage of funds for financing small businesses. However, what is more often the case is that many small business owners are unfamiliar with the range of sources of funds and financial services available to them.

Another common complaint is that banks and other financial institutions insist on 100% guarantees of the success of a new small business venture. But the problem is that they are not provided with sufficient documented information to make a positive decision.

Therefore, being prepared, understanding the procedures involved, and being familiar with the different types of financing available are the first steps in demonstrating good management of a financial proposal.

You should also understand that banks and other financial institutions are no different than you — they are in competition with each other in the same way you will be with your competitors.

Banks make money by lending money at a profit. If they don't lend money, they don't make that profit. If you don't sell your goods or services, you won't make a profit. However, for business to be profitable to the bank, the bank has to assess the risk in lending its money.

In borrowing money, the words risk and interest are closely connected. Risk is the degree of danger the lender has in losing funds loaned to you. Interest is what you pay a lender for the use of borrowed funds. Normally, the higher the risk, the higher the interest rate.

Bankers' decisions are based on their judgment of the viability of your proposal. This judgment uses no secret formulas (banks do make errors in lending money that they cannot collect). However, bankers do use certain basic information to determine risk and make decisions. This information is discussed in the following sections.

c. PREPARING THE PAPERWORK

The style and content of a loan application are of major importance when asking for a loan. To make the best impression on those you approach for funding, it is critical to have all the facts properly documented. Regardless of the type of loan, the information required by the lender is basically the same.

The lender wants to know who you are, what your plans are, and what these plans will do for the business. Preparing this information, and the analysis that backs it up, is quite simple. A systematic approach includes the following steps.

1. Resume of the owner

The lender wants to know something about you (and any other owner or owners), such as your education and experience (or lack of it) and how these are valuable to the business.

The lender wants to be assured of your managerial skills. A past track record demonstrating ability in matters such as production, marketing, financing, and similar

areas and how these can be related to the business you propose starting are some determining factors in assessing your management ability.

In essence, the lender needs this information to size up your character, and to assess your honesty, reliability, trustworthiness, responsibility, willingness to work, and ability to use borrowed funds wisely.

The lender can then assess the relative strengths of your management abilities based on his or her experience lending money to other businesses.

2. Personal financial information

If you do not have a previous business track record, the lender will probably need personal financial information about you and any other owners. This information shows the lender what other financial support you can fall back on if the business is not immediately successful and requires further owner investment. A bank personal financial information form is illustrated in Sample #9.

3. References

You probably need to provide references, both personal and business. If you have dealt with other banks previously, references from them can be helpful, including details of any previous or outstanding loans. Your accountant and lawyer are also useful as references.

4. Products and/or services

The lender will want some details about the products and services of your proposed company. This includes information concerning products, their prices, and their quality in comparison with competitors.

The lender is concerned with such matters as the acceptability of your business's products, their diversity, their competitiveness, and the possible problems of borrowed money going into risky new products.

68

SAMPLE #9
PERSONAL FINANCIAL INFORMATION FORM

TO: BIG BANK

LAST NAME | FIRST NAME | INITIAL

ADDRESS | APT. NO. | HOME TELEPHONE | BUSINESS TELEPHONE

POSTAL CODE | BIRTHPLACE

MARITAL STATUS:
[ ] SINGLE [ ] DIVORCED
[ ] MARRIED [ ] SEPARATED

DATE OF BIRTH: DAY | MONTH | YEAR

SPOUSE FIRST NAME | NO. DEPENDENTS

AT PRESENT ADDRESS FOR ____ YEARS
[ ] OWN [ ] RENT $ ____ PER MONTH

PREVIOUS ADDRESS IF AT ABOVE LESS THAN 2 YEARS

EMPLOYMENT AND INCOME

EMPLOYER (NAME AND ADDRESS) | OCCUPATION | HOW LONG | GROSS ANNUAL EARNINGS $

PREVIOUS EMPLOYER (IF WITH ABOVE LESS THAN 2 YEARS) | OCCUPATION | HOW LONG | GROSS ANNUAL EARNINGS $

SPOUSE NOW EMPLOYED BY (NAME AND ADDRESS) | OCCUPATION | HOW LONG | GROSS ANNUAL EARNINGS $

OTHER FAMILY INCOME $
SOURCE:

ACCOUNTS AT THIS BRANCH:
[ ] LOCATION OF OTHER ACCOUNTS OR
[ ] PREVIOUS BANK IF NEW ACCOUNT

NAME AND ADDRESS OF NEAREST RELATIVE NOT LIVING WITH ME/US. | TELEPHONE | RELATIONSHIP

INVESTMENTS (STOCKS, BONDS, TERM DEPOSITS, LIFE INSURANCE)

TYPE	COMPANY/ISSUER	FACE VALUE/UNITS	MARKET VALUE	IF ASSIGNED, WHO TO?

INSTALLMENT ACCOUNTS/DEBTS OWING

OWING TO	NAME/ACCOUNT NUMBER	PURPOSE	OWING SINCE	ORIGINAL AMOUNT	NOW OWING	MONTHLY PAYMENT
THIS OR OTHER BANKS FINANCE COMPANIES OR CREDIT UNIONS				$	$	$
CHARGE ACCOUNTS						
CHARGEX/VISA						
			TOTAL			

IF NEW LOAN ACCOUNT, RECORD IDENTIFICATION DETAILS (e.g. DRIVER'S LICENCE NUMBER)

IF RESIDENCE OWNED, DESCRIBE:
[ ] DETACHED [ ] SEMI [ ] TOWN HOUSE [ ] CONDOMINIUM

YEAR PURCH	PRESENT VALUE	TAXES PAID	MONTHLY PAYMENTS (P.I.T.)

MORTGAGES OWING TO | MATURES | PRESENT AMOUNT

REGISTERED OWNER(S) | FIRE INSURANCE $

OTHER PROPERTY OWNED | MTGE AMT $ | NET EQUITY $

FINANCIAL POSITION SUMMARY

ASSETS
BANK ACCOUNTS $
REAL ESTATE
STOCKS AND BONDS
LIFE INSURANCE, ETC. (CASH VALUE)
CAR — YEAR — MAKE — MODEL
OTHER
TOTAL ASSETS $

LIABILITIES
INSTALLMENT ACCOUNTS/DEBTS (AS SHOWN) $
AMOUNT OF MORTGAGES OWING (AS ABOVE)
INCOME TAXES OWING
REAL ESTATE TAXES
OTHER
TOTAL LIABILITIES $
NET WORTH $

THE ABOVE INFORMATION IS PROVIDED TO THE BANK AS A FCTUAL STATEMENT OF MY AFFAIRS.
YOU MAY AT ANY TIME OBTAIN INFORMATION ABOUT ME FROM MY EMPLOYER, ANY CREDIT BUREAU OR ANY OTHER PERSON IN CONNECTION WITH ANY OF MY DEALINGS WITH YOU, IN ADDITION, YOU MAY DISCLOSE INFORMATION AND DOCUMENTS RELATING TO MY CREDIT HISTORY WITH YOU TO ANY CREDIT BUREAU, TO ANY PERSON WITH WHOM I HAVE OR PROPOSE TO HAVE FINANCIAL DEALINGS, OR IF YOU BELIEVE THAT THE DISCLOSURE IS REQUIRED BY LAW.

_____ SIGNATURE

_____ SIGNATURE

With reference to future prospects, the bank might want to consider the impact of environmental and/or technological change on your business. Such factors as the availability of labor (if it is a labor intensive business), consistency of supply of products or items to be sold, and the adequacy of the premises to meet your projected sales are of concern to the lender.

An assessment of your market and potential market share could be included at this point. If your market plan is professionally prepared, include it here.

Finally, don't be reticent about including the names of your nearest competitors.

5. Financial statements

Financial statement projections are required for the next 12 months with detailed calculations showing, in particular, how total annual sales are calculated and the projected operating costs. Forecast cash flow projections, month by month, for the next year is also required.

In other words, the lender is interested in how your business is expected to do and, most important, from projected cash flow, its ability to repay any loans.

In particular, the lender is looking for potential problems indicated by your financial statements. These problems could be matters such as proposing to extend too much credit, too high an inventory in relation to sales, too high a proposed dividend payout or owner cash withdrawals, a serious possible decline in sales in poor economic times, or too much investment in fixed assets in relation to sales.

The amount of your investment or equity in the business is important. Banks and other lending institutions do not finance 100% of the money needed by a new business. You have to put some of your own money in — as much as 25% of the total cash required. If you are not prepared to risk your own money, why should the bank risk its funds?

You might like to show how the required money is going to be used, and the various sources of funding. A very simple plan would look like this:

Use of funds		Source of funds	
Inventory	$25,000	Bank loan	$45,000
Equipment/ fixtures	23,000	Shareholder loan	8,000
Contingencies	5,000	Total	$53,000
Total	$53,000		

6. Security offered

The prospective lender will want details of the security offered for any loan. This includes a description of the assets (land, building, equipment, and fixtures). If you can offer personal securities (house, stocks, bonds, life insurance, and similar items), these, too, should be listed.

In particular, if there has been a recent appraisal made on the land and building, this is useful to indicate the property's worth.

If the land and/or building are not owned, your lease agreement might form the security offered. In such a case, provide a copy of the lease agreement to the lender with a statement from the lessor showing that all rent payments already made (if any) have been made promptly.

7. Insurance policies

The lender will want to know if the business is adequately insured against losses and liabilities and, in each case, who the beneficiaries are. Therefore, make copies of any insurance policies available to the lender.

d. FORMAL LOAN PLAN LAYOUT

Sample #10 is an outline of a possible loan plan. Many financial lenders do not need this type of formal outline but are quite satisfied with the answers to the questions

SAMPLE #10
LOAN PLAN

A. INTRODUCTION

1. Nature of your business
2. Major products/services and their sources
3. Location and its pros/cons
4. Brief description of your market/clientele
5. Market trends (stability and growth) and how affected by the economy
6. Your advantages/disadvantages over competitors
7. Organizational form (proprietorship, partnership, or limited company)

B. FINANCIAL

1. Reason for loan and amount required
2. Proposed terms of repayment
3. Amount of equity investment
4. Security or collateral for loan

C. PERSONAL INFORMATION

1. Your education and business background
2. Credit references (banker, lawyer, accountant)
3. Name(s) of financial institutions dealt with before, any loans made, how they were repaid
4. Personal income tax statements for past 3 years
5. Personal financial statements
6. Summary of business background

D. BUSINESS INFORMATION

1. Marketing plan
2. Pricing policy
3. Credit policy
4. Advertising policy

E. FINANCIAL PROJECTIONS

1. Proposed opening day balance sheet
2. Sales and expense projections for next 12 months, by month
3. Cash flow projections for next 12 months, by month
4. Proposed balance sheet one year hence

(Any necessary explanations should be included with these projections and if there is more than one principal partner/shareholder, some of the personal information will have to be provided for each one.)

discussed above. But there may be occasions when it may be advantageous to use the following format.

The importance of careful preparation of all the paperwork cannot be overstressed. The manner in which this information is professionally prepared and presented to a potential lender goes a long way toward ensuring that the required funds are obtained.

In calculations of sales and expenses, accuracy is critical. If careless errors are made in overestimating revenue or underestimating expenses (thus producing a "padded" profit amount), your credibility will be damaged and your chances of obtaining borrowed funds will be considerably decreased. For this reason, professional help from an accountant may be necessary.

Even though a suggested list of paperwork items has been outlined above, it might be a good idea to contact potential lenders, in each specific case, to determine what they would like to have. This ensures that time is not wasted putting together a report that is far more than a lender is interested in or that fails to include specifics that the lender does want.

When seeking financing it is a good idea to make appointments in a businesslike way with each potential lender. That is more likely to portray the image of a professional business operator than simply walking in the door and asking for money.

e. LENDING DECISIONS

When you apply for funds, there are two possibilities: your application will be approved or rejected.

1. Approval

If a request for financing is approved, find out about the conditions, terms, payment methods, interest rates, security requirements, and if there are any front-end charges or fees. Don't accept the financing until you receive and understand all this information and its impact on the proposed business.

If financing is approved only under certain conditions, determine if these conditions are severe enough to restrict the operating standards you desire. Will the conditions commit you to more than was intended, or are they normal financing requirements that were simply overlooked?

Once a final commitment is arranged, it is a good idea to provide the lender with copies of future financial statements. Frequently this is a requirement for obtaining funding. Even if it is not, financial statements provide the lender with progress reports about the business and will help the lender process future applications for further financing.

2. Rejection

If a request for financing is not approved, find out why. Use the lender's experience to advantage. He or she has a reason for not providing the financing. Lenders handle many requests for financing and have experience in the financial aspects (even if they do not have direct management experience) of many businesses.

For example, the lender might be able to see that your business will run into a shortage of working capital with the financial plan proposed. A shortage of working capital is one of the common reasons for failure of many retail businesses. If your business is in trouble because you are short working capital, it is often difficult to obtain additional working capital assistance. It is far preferable to ask for additional funds to strengthen working capital at the outset. A lender may be able to point out possible problems in this area in your proposed financing plan.

If there is something else wrong with the financing proposal, see if it can be corrected and then reapply. If not, use this knowledge when approaching other potential lenders, or on future occasions when seeking funds.

Once you have exhausted most normal channels of financing, such as banks, commercial finance companies, consumer finance companies, and even credit unions, you could still pursue the following possible sources of money.

f. SMALL BUSINESS ADMINISTRATION (U.S.)

In the U.S., if all else fails, you might want to consider the Small Business Administration (SBA). The SBA was created in 1953 by the U.S. federal government to succeed several preceding agencies responsible for assisting entrepreneurs. Since that date, SBA has endured and expanded to embrace many activities. Its functions include finance and investment, among others.

The SBA is organized into 10 regions and each region is subdivided, providing district or branch offices in many diverse centers of population. As the lender of final resort, the SBA tries not to compete with or replace the private banking system but to supplement it.

Present SBA guidelines defining who qualifies for small business assistance vary, depending on the general classification of the enterprise. At present, the eligibility of a business is measured by sales volume or revenue. For example, the upper limit on sales ranges from $3.5 million to $17 million depending on the specific type of business.

Loans made by SBA generally mature in 10 years or less for fixtures and equipment, and are repaid in equal monthly installments of principal and interest, although this time period may be extended to 25 years where the purchase concerns land and/or a building.

Working capital loans can be made for periods up to seven years. Regardless of the loan term, the loan may be repaid at any time prior to maturity without penalty.

Since the SBA's regulations change from time to time, you should verify current conditions by contacting your nearest branch of the SBA (listed in your telephone directory under U.S. Government) or write to:

Small Business Administration
Washington, D.C. 20416

g. GOVERNMENT FINANCING IN CANADA

The Small Businesses Loans Act (SBLA) lends up to $100,000 to small businesses whose annual gross sales are not over $2 million. The rate of interest is 1% over the prime lending rate and the maximum term is 10 years. The loan cannot be used for working capital.

All chartered banks and Alberta Treasury Branches are authorized to make loans under the SBLA. In addition, loans may be made by credit unions, caisses populaires, or other cooperative societies, trust companies, loan companies, and insurance companies which have applied and been designated as lenders under the act.

Therefore, if all other sources fail, talk to your own banker or other lender about the SBLA, and obtain a credit application. If you want further information about SBLA, write to:

Small Businesses Loans Administration
Department of Regional Industrial
Expansion
235 Queen Street
Ottawa, ON
K1A 0H5

In Canada, you should also be aware of the Federal Business Development Bank, or FBDB. This lender is sometimes referred to as the lender of last resort. It was established by the government especially to help those companies that could not obtain financing elsewhere. If your funding application has been turned down by other financial institutions, you may apply to the FBDB.

To obtain FBDB financing, the amount of your investment in the business must generally be sufficient to ensure that you are committed to it and that the business may reasonably be expected to be successful.

Financing from the FBDB can range from a few thousand dollars to $100,000. Not many loans are made in excess of that amount. The amount that can be borrowed for a specific purpose depends on your ability to satisfy the bank's general requirements and repayment conditions are usually tied to your cash flow.

The FBDB also offers management counselling, management training, and other business information services including Counselling Assistance for Small Enterprise (CASE).

The purpose of CASE is to assist owners and managers of small businesses improve their methods of doing business. To be eligible you can already be, or about to be, established in business in Canada. One restriction is that you must not have more than 75 full-time employees. There is also a nominal daily charge for their service. If you wish to pursue this, contact your local branch of the FBDB, or write to:

Federal Business Development Bank
800 Victoria Square
Tour de la Place - Victoria
P.O. Box 335
Montreal, PQ
H4Z 1L4

14
FRANCHISING

You might want to consider the franchising route to starting a new retail business. Franchising as a means for the independent entrepreneur to go into business has been booming for the last 20 years and there appears to be no immediate letup in sight.

You only need to look at popular business journals and newspaper business sections, or even in the business opportunities section of newspaper classified advertising to see the many references to franchised businesses.

Franchising is simply a form of distribution of goods or services. Because of its high profile in the fast food industry, it is often identified primarily with that type of business. But we all use many other types of franchise goods or services each day without even realizing it.

a. A DEFINITION OF FRANCHISING

There is no commonly accepted definition of franchising that can be applied in all cases. However, in general terms it is a method of distribution or marketing in which a company (the franchisor) grants by contract to an individual or another company (the franchisee) the right to carry on a business in a prescribed way in a particular location for a specified period.

The franchisee may be allowed to operate only one establishment, or may be given an area in which a number of franchised outlets may be operated. That area could be a city, a province or state, a major portion of the country, or indeed the whole country. For example, a few years ago, Wendy's in the U.S. gave a private Canadian company the territorial rights to all of Canada for Wendy's restaurant operations.

For the services that it provides, the franchisor receives a fee, or royalty, usually based on gross sales, or else a fixed fee (for example, a flat monthly or annual amount, or a fixed fee based on the number of rooms in a hotel or motel franchise).

In addition, the franchisee usually has to pay a share of local, regional, or national advertising costs. Again, this advertising cost is usually a percentage of sales revenue. The fees and other costs are generally payable monthly.

For what you pay as a franchisee you may receive business advice, financial aid (direct or indirect), market research, lease negotiation, site evaluation, building plans, training programs, national advertising, an accounting system, and an established and widely recognized name and image.

Although you must provide or arrange for most of the financing required, the franchisor may provide some of this initial capital. In such cases, the monthly fee will probably include an extra amount to pay back this financing with interest.

b. ADVANTAGES TO THE FRANCHISEE

Some of the major advantages to taking the franchise route into business are:

(a) It is possible to start up as a generally independent entrepreneur, but with the support of an established parent company: the franchisor. The franchisor may provide you with assistance in such matters as obtaining financing, site selection, building construction supervision, employee training, and support during the difficult break-in period subsequent to opening.

(b) As a franchisee you have the opportunity to buy into an established concept, although this, by itself, is no guarantee that you will succeed. However, the risk of failure is generally reduced. Statistics show that the independent retailer opening a small business has only a 20% to 30% chance of surviving the first few critical years. For franchisees, similar statistics show there is an 80% chance of success.

(c) You have the ongoing backup of the franchisor, who can provide assistance and help solve problems since he or she can afford to hire specialists in the head office in such areas as cost control, marketing and sales, and research and development.

(d) The franchisor can provide the potential for local, regional, or even national advertising (albeit at a cost to you).

(e) You have access to credit that you may not otherwise have. Banks and similar lending institutions are usually more willing to lend money to an entrepreneur who has the backing of a successful franchisor than to the completely independent retailer.

(f) You may be able to purchase supplies at a reduced cost since the franchisor can purchase in bulk and pass the savings on to the franchisees (as much as 3% to 6% on costs may be saved this way).

(g) You may find an opportunity to take over a turnkey franchise operation. A turnkey operation is one where the franchisor provides you with a completely set up franchise, performing services such as assistance in obtaining financing, site evaluation, selection and acquisition, construction and equipping of premises, training you and your staff, provision of "start-up" assistance, purchasing the initial inventory, providing management and accounting reporting systems, providing advertising, public relations and marketing services, and, after opening, ongoing supervision and guidance. In other words, about all you have to do is turn the key in the door and you're in business.

(h) Finally, franchising offers many of the advantages of an integrated chain business (without some of the disadvantages) because of the voluntary nature of the contract rather than central ownership.

c. DISADVANTAGES TO THE FRANCHISEE

Here are some disadvantages to franchising that you must consider.

(a) The cost of the services provided by the franchisor comes off the top of your sales revenue and could add up to 10% or more of that revenue.

(b) Even though the franchise arrangement allows you to start a business that you might otherwise only be able to begin with difficulty, there is a loss of freedom since you must adhere to the franchisor's standards and you may have limited scope for personal initiative.

(c) In some cases, the markup that the franchisor adds to the products that you must buy from him or her can increase your operating costs, particularly if an equally good product could be purchased locally at a lower cost.

(d) Experience shows that you run some risk of not achieving the sales potential, and thus the profit, that the franchisor stated was possible when selling the franchise.

(e) If the franchisor operates from a jurisdiction other than the one in which you have the franchise, and his or her obligations are not fulfilled, it can be difficult, if not impossible, to seek redress.

d. BEFORE PROCEEDING

Do not be lured into buying a franchise by quick profits, minimum effort, low initial investment, and freedom to be your own boss. Too many entrepreneurs disregard warning lights when evaluating a franchise, push aside sensible (generally negative) advice, and fail to completely examine the franchisor or the contract, even when the franchisor suggests that this be done.

Some franchisees end up doing very well, but by far the majority find themselves working harder than they anticipated under contract arrangements that may seem harsh or restrictive since they do not provide the anticipated return on investment. Some of these entrepreneurs fail, since they expected too much from too little effort on their part.

If you would like further information on franchising, see *Franchising in the U.S.* or *Franchising in Canada,* two other titles in the Self-Counsel Series.

In any case, do not sign a franchise contract until you have carefully investigated the franchisor and have had a lawyer check the contract for you.

15
LAYOUT AND SELLING

With arrangements for financing underway, it is not too early to think about the layout of your store and training your sales employees with the objective of maximizing sales. Your store layout is a critical factor in merchandising your products.

Although this chapter is primarily concerned with the internal layout of your retail store and the need for having trained employees, the external appearance of your shop can have an important bearing on whether customers are attracted inside.

a. EXTERNAL APPEARANCE

Potential customers particularly judge your store on their initial reaction to its external appearance.

External appearance covers the obvious factors of state of repair and cleanliness (for example, paint or other exterior wall covering) as well as the cleanliness of your sidewalk. The sidewalk should be kept clear of dust, dirt, trash, snow, and slush at all times.

1. Signs

External signs should also be kept in good condition. These external signs should be straightforward and simple and not too wordy. A sign should communicate simply and briefly the type of business you are in and the type of products or services you offer. Keep in mind whether it is to be read by passing motorists or pedestrians, or both.

If your sign also has to be read at night, make sure that sign lighting will do the job intended.

Before contracting for or erecting any external sign, check that there are no limitations imposed by the municipality or your shopping center rental contract. It is expensive to have a sign produced that you cannot use because it is larger than allowed.

2. Window display

The external appearance of your shop also includes what the customer can see of the inside of your store from outside, such as the window display.

This display should be kept current (i.e., regular display rotation as frequently as every two weeks) with fresh price or other eye-catching signs that are professionally prepared, not felt penned on an old square of cardboard. Keep your display free of clutter. It is better to have fewer items in your display, but make it attractive.

Consider your window as a stage when planning displays. In other words, the center foreground is the location of your prime display items with the sides and rear for secondary displays.

Take advantage of themes, seasons, holidays, and other events to make your display interesting and appealing. An interesting display can attract window shoppers into your store and turn them into purchasers.

If display lights are used, plan lighting carefully to minimize window glare. Do not have spotlights shining outward to dazzle window shoppers.

Keep your windows clean. Dirty windows can be detrimental to attracting customers. As much as possible keep your window clear of signs. Glass is made to see through, although there are occasions when "sale" signs are needed to attract the customers' attention.

Remember, a window display is part of your business's promotion. The attractiveness of the exterior of your store, including the window display, is especially important if you are opening in premises that are new or in an outlet that previously provided different products and/or services. The exterior must tell potential customers that you are new and that you have something special to offer them.

b. INTERIOR

The exterior of your store may help attract some customers, but it is the interior decor and atmosphere, combined with the assistance and attitude of sales persons that can convert those potential customers into purchasers. The interior of your store, like the exterior, must be compatible with your products and services and the image you are trying to portray.

When you look for an appropriate site for your store, you should ensure that it has adequate interior space for sufficient inventory, an area for an office, and possibly even a receiving and shipping area.

You should also consider the necessity for adequate space for expansion when business improves. For example, if you are considering expansion, the space for inventory should be more than adequate to take care of today's inventory needs as well as providing room for inventory as business increases.

1. Layout

Layout is probably one of the most critical factors in retail merchandising. The objective in retailing is to sell, and the way a store is laid out can be extremely effective in maximizing sales.

The layout of any store depends on the amount of space available and the type of products or services offered. For example, a grocery store will have a completely different type of display and layout from a clothing store. The clothing store has to allow space for fitting rooms. However, in all cases, the objective is to effectively display merchandise.

In very small stores, layout is inflexible. A counter, at which one or more employees work, separates customers from the entire merchandise display that is behind the counter.

In larger stores, there may be more display areas around the remaining walls. In even larger stores, there may be counters or rack displays around which customers must circulate to select items. In such cases, layout can be important.

2. Aisles

Main aisles should be provided as customers enter the main door(s) since that is where the heaviest traffic is. The counters on either side of a main aisle are generally more effective than subsidiary aisles in catching your customers' attention. Subsidiary aisles, if there are any, should be off to the sides.

Counters at either end of aisles are also good spots for catching attention and are good locations for special displays, sale items, new items, loss leaders, and similar goods.

All aisles should be as wide as is practical to minimize crowding and better display the merchandise. Displays in the aisles should be planned where possible with knowledge about the buying habits of your customers.

There are basically two types of retail store customer: those who know what they want when they come into the store and seek it out or ask for it immediately, and those who are just browsers without specific buying objectives but who might buy something if it appeals to them.

Studies show that browsers tend to move counterclockwise around a store, while those knowing what they want tend to move clockwise after entering the store. If you can categorize the majority of your customers as being of one type or the other, you may be able to plan your interior displays to advantage.

3. Fixtures and equipment

Use display fixtures and equipment that complement the decor of your interior. However, if you have only a limited budget for fixtures, you may be wiser to purchase or rent less expensive fixtures rather than cut back on the amount of inventory on display. It is selling inventory (not the quality of your display fixtures and equipment) that provides you with profit and cash flow.

4. Displays

Do not overcrowd displays. Too crowded a display can confuse customers and may prevent them from easily spotting something they are looking for or would buy if it were more obviously visible. A choice between two or three similar products is easier and more likely than if five or six are on display.

Group displays into obvious categories and, if your customers are generally repeat ones (as they might be, for example, in a grocery store) do not constantly move products to different locations since that can irritate customers.

Try to create an air of spaciousness in displays and wherever possible avoid displays that block the view of other parts of the store or location of cashiers.

The objective of good display is to make the items most customers want stand out. Display signs, where appropriate, can help, but don't overdo them since that can detract from the actual merchandise displays. Poor signs detract, so have them professionally done.

If you advertise (for example, on the radio or in the newspaper) that you have a sale on certain items, special sale signs should highlight the location of those items.

Sign colors are important for visual impact. Sale signs are often red letters with a yellow background. But black or red letters on white also stand out well.

5. Environment

Make good use of light, ventilation, and heat for customer and employee comfort. Comfortable conditions must exist for customers and for the employees who serve them. Without pleasant surroundings, customers can be discouraged and unhappy employees can add further discouragement.

Use colors on walls, ceiling, and floor coverings with discretion. Bold colors can appear aggressive and inappropriate except in special situations. Colors that blend in well are preferable in most cases since they should serve primarily as a backdrop to your merchandise displays and should not overwhelm them.

However, some bright colors (such as orange, yellow, or even white) in moderate amounts can be helpful in highlighting some lower priced merchandise.

6. Non-selling activities

You should separate selling from non-selling activities. In other words, keep accounting areas, credit offices, public telephones, and similar functions separate from the main function of the store — selling merchandise. Generally, these non-selling functions should be at the back of the shop since the front of any store is prime selling space.

7. Use of space

Use space effectively. Know the value of your space and locate merchandise accordingly.

Prime merchandise (for example, items that have the highest profit) should be near the front of the store since that space is the most valuable. It is here in the highest traffic area that impulse merchandise and convenience goods should be located.

Cash register stands are also good locations for impulse items. Place sale merchandise or other special items in a wide aisle in a special display "obstacle" rack for effective merchandising. Customers will become used to looking for specials in that particular location.

Specialists in store layout say that the front third of a store should provide 50% of total sales, and the back two-thirds the remaining 50%.

c. SHOPLIFTING

These days, retailers must be increasingly concerned with shoplifting. One way to discourage such theft is to train employees to be alert and, in particular, to offer to help customers the moment they enter the store. Businesses that are firm in prosecuting shoplifters may also earn a community reputation that discourages potential shoplifters.

However, despite these measures, more precaution is usually necessary. For example, direct customer access to more expensive items should be limited with an employee in attendance who must unlock a display case or rack to remove an item for customer inspection.

Another method is to install a device or tag on the item that is difficult, if not impossible, for the customer to remove (there are various types of these tags). If an item leaves the store with the device or tag still attached, it triggers an alarm at any exit and alerts employees to a potential shoplifter. Only if an item is paid for at the sales counter is the alarm device or tag be removed.

Despite these precautions, shoplifting continues, and it is unfortunate that its cost must be passed on in the form of higher prices to the honest customers.

d. SELLING

To be successful, every idea, product, or service has to be sold. The selling process is one of encouraging or persuading the transfer of products or services from one person or company to another. Selling is an important aspect of every retail business.

In order to be sold, a product or service must satisfy a basic want or need of a customer. Although customers can sometimes be sold something they do not really want, this does not benefit the retailer in the long run since it does not provide repeat business or word-of-mouth advertising.

1. Salespeople and product knowledge

The major factors to consider in establishing an effective team of sale employees are the specific skills and technical knowledge that may be required in your retail business. Frequently, these skills relate to product knowledge.

Employees must be adequately trained, where necessary, in each product's use. They must know its value, as well as its strengths and weaknesses. They should be able to answer these questions:

(a) What are its uses?

(b) How does it compare with similar products?

(c) What are its advantages and disadvantages?

(d) Is the product high quality and thus high priced, or low priced because of low quality?

(e) Does the product provide value for money?

A good salesperson who has product knowledge can convert that knowledge into sales that benefit the customer, the salesperson, and your business.

To be sold, a product must be well presented or displayed. This presentation includes the way the product is packaged or wrapped to show its features, ease of usage, and advantages or benefits.

2. General skills

The customer perceives sales employees as if they were you, the owner of the business. Therefore, incompetent, indifferent, or impolite clerks can create serious ill will for your business, even if all other factors about your business are in place to make it successful.

Sales employees must be outgoing and people-oriented. A pleasant attitude toward customers and fellow employees is critical. In addition, attentiveness and tidiness are appropriate characteristics for them to have even if your business is essentially a self-serve one. Even in a self-serve business, customers frequently want a sales employee to provide answers to questions or to help the customer decide to purchase particular products or to suggest alternatives.

Salespeople must be trained to find out as much as they can about potential customers prior to making a sale. This can be done by observation and/or conversation with the customer.

The information obtained often indicates how to make a sales approach that is positive to gain the attention of the customer, to make sure the customer is made aware of a need, and to ensure the product is properly presented.

This presentation should be enthusiastic and in good taste. Any claims or statements made about the product should be truthful. Warranties and/or guarantees should be explained. Salespeople should be prepared to overcome any objections the prospective customer may have to the products.

The final step in the selling process is "closing." Closing is getting the customer to decide to buy. This includes more than just getting the customer to say yes; it also means providing a level of service that will ensure future orders and sales.

16
PURCHASING

Each time you purchase inventory or supplies for your retail business, a cost is incurred. To minimize these costs, pay close attention to the purchasing function. Effective purchasing usually reduces overall costs. To illustrate, consider the following:

Sales	$1,000,000
Cost of sales	400,000
Other costs	550,000
Net profit	$ 50,000

If the business in the above situation could save 1/2 of 1% through more effective purchasing of its inventory (cost of goods sold), it would be a savings of $2,000 (1/2% x $400,000). Assuming no other costs change, profit would thus increase from $50,000 to $52,000 — an increase in profit of 4%!

The purpose of purchasing, whether by you or someone you delegate, is to make sure inventory and other supplies and services are available in quantities appropriate to predetermined standards, at the right price, and at a minimum cost to meet desired standards.

The person responsible for purchasing, regardless of the size of business, can benefit from applying some of the basic purchasing practices and procedures discussed in this chapter. This benefit is particularly true when there are shortages of products with resulting high prices.

By having and following established purchasing procedures, you can avoid purchasing pitfalls such as panic buying, over- or short-purchasing, buying by price rather than by a combination of quality and price, pressure buying, or, what is quite common, "satisfied buying." Satisfied buying means the purchaser buys with the assumption that no improvements in either quality or price can be achieved.

a. SELECTING SUPPLIERS

It is possible in your business that you have only one product that you buy from one supplier at one price and sell at another. However, in most businesses it is normal to deal with several suppliers, whether they are manufacturers or wholesalers.

The important consideration in selecting suppliers is to contact as many of them as is practical to ensure that enough quotations are received so that the right quality of product is purchased at the lowest possible price. A minimum of three quotations is recommended for each product or service, although this may not be necessary or possible in every case. In some cases, you will want these quotations in writing. In other cases, you might take them over the telephone.

You should keep the number of suppliers to a minimum to save on ordering, bookkeeping, errors, time spent with suppliers' representatives, and possible overlapping or duplicating of inventory items.

Also, if you spread your business over too many suppliers, your account will simply be too small with each of them to gain their attention or benefit from quantity discounts or other supplier services.

Don't consider your suppliers as simply sources of inventory. Find out if they have retailer assistance programs. Some manufacturers offer marketing, sales, or promotional aids; national cooperative advertising; merchandising guidelines; and other help for more profitable store management. The quantity and quality of such services can be as important to your profits as the merchandise they sell you.

1. Product knowledge

In order to choose the right supplier, you have to have product knowledge. What products or goods are available that will help you manage your business profitably?

There are a number of different ways of obtaining product knowledge.

(a) Sales representatives are probably the most useful source of product knowledge. The biggest problem for the retailer is finding enough time to talk to all sales representatives and separate the useful information they provide from inflated claims about their products.

(b) Suppliers' printed information (brochures and bulletins) are often prepared by product manufacturers and some dealers to describe new products they have available. Seek only specific facts in this printed information and ignore comments that exaggerate the product's good qualities. Some large manufacturers produce catalogues of all their products, both old and new.

(c) Advertisements in trade magazines and journals are another valuable source of product knowledge. These advertisements are convenient since you can see them while looking through the journal and know they are directed specifically at your type of business. They provide information that might not otherwise be available to you if there are no sales representatives or dealers for that product in your area.

(d) Conventions and trade shows, if held for your type of business, provide an opportunity to discuss a variety of different products or services with their manufacturers or suppliers within a short space of time. The representatives can give demonstrations and explain details about their products, quote prices, take orders, and be of help in other ways.

2. Purchasing arrangements

There are a number of different types of purchasing arrangements possible with suppliers. Here are some:

(a) Competitive or open market buying where quotations are received by telephone, in person directly from a salesperson, or in writing through the mail. Wherever possible, written quotations are preferable.

(b) Single source buying is common when the product you want to sell is so unique that there is only one readily available manufacturer/supplier. In such cases, you may have little control over the cost of the product.

(c) Contract buying might be used for a product or products that need to be purchased in relatively large quantities over a fairly long period (for example, from three months to a year) to ensure a steady supply and the manufacturer or supplier can guarantee the price during this period. However, some long-term contracts may allow for possible negotiated price changes (within a specified range) during the term of the contract.

(d) One-stop buying occurs when a business buys all, or a majority, of its required products from one supplier. For example, a restaurant owner might buy all food and other supplies from one supplier. There is only one order required, only one delivery, and only one invoice to pay. Theoretically this reduces purchasing costs. However, since there may be no competitive bidding with one-stop buying, the financial advantages have to be carefully weighed before using this purchase method.

3. Ethical purchasing

Purchasing practices with suppliers must be ethical. For example, it would be unfair to ask a supplier to quote on an order if there is little or no likelihood of that supplier receiving the order.

Similarly, assuming the quality meets the standards you require, it is normal to give the order to the supplier with the lowest price. If this is not done, suppliers will soon learn that a low price quotation is not worth it and begin quoting higher prices.

Also, it is not considered ethical to force a supplier to lower prices with the promise of additional later orders, since that practice will eventually reach a point of no return with suppliers unwilling to do business with you.

4. Purchase orders

If your business is large enough, you may want to use purchase orders.

A purchase order describes the product, and gives the specifications (where necessary) and the quoted price. Three copies of the purchase order are required: one for the supplier, one for the person responsible for receiving, and the third for accounting purposes to be attached to the invoice when it is received with payment. A typical purchase order is illustrated in Sample #11.

If orders are placed by telephone they should be followed up as soon as possible with the purchase order or other written confirmation.

b. RECEIVING GOODS

The last step in the purchasing route is receiving the goods. The person designated for this job must be knowledgeable about the products being received. In a smaller business, that might be the business owner.

In larger businesses, there may be a separate receiving department responsible for checking all deliveries before distributing the items to the individual departments or storage areas.

In all cases, where purchase orders have been prepared, a copy of the purchase order should be on hand during the receiving process. In particular, quantities received should be checked against quantities ordered and invoiced.

Wherever items are purchased by weight, appropriate weighing scales should be provided so that delivered weight can be verified against invoice weight.

Finally, prices on invoices should be checked against the quotation references or against the purchase order.

Quality control tests may need to be performed to ensure that the quality of delivered items meets the specifications. Any damage to delivered goods should be reported immediately to the supplier for adjustment.

All delivery slips (or invoices if they accompany the deliveries) should be stamped and the stamp should be initialled in the appropriate spots to indicate that all the required checking has been completed. A typical receiving stamp is illustrated in Sample #12.

By insisting that the employee responsible for checking deliveries stamp each delivery slip or invoice and initial where necessary, you help instill a sense of responsibility for the delivery.

HAROLD'S HARDWARE
60 South Street, Hometown
Telephone: (261) 434-5734

PURCHASE ORDER   #619

(The purchase order number must appear on all invoices, bills of lading
or correspondence relating to this purchase. The invoice must accompany shipment).

Department _____

Purchase order date _____   Delivery Date _____

To suppliers: _____

Description	Quantity	Price

Purchasing Manager's signature _____

SAMPLE #12
RECEIVING STAMP

RECEIVING STAMP

Date received _____

Quantity checked by _____

Quality checked by _____

Prices checked by _____

Listed on receiving report by _____

SAMPLE #13
CREDIT MEMORANDUM

CREDIT MEMORANDUM

Supplier _____ Date _____

Please issue a credit memorandum for the following:

Quantity	Item description	Unit cost	Total

Reason for request for credit:

Delivery driver's signature _____

If goods are short-shipped, or returned to the supplier for any reason, it is a good idea to fill in a credit memo and have the delivery driver sign it. This is your proof that the goods should not be paid for and ensures that the supplier issues you an appropriate credit invoice. A credit memo is illustrated in Sample #13.

c. TIMING PURCHASES AND PAYMENTS

Wherever possible, take advantage of a supplier's billing practices. Most companies supply goods as required during a month and within a few days of the month end mail you a statement for that month.

Suppose you buy a month's supply of items from a supplier at the beginning of each month, using the items as required during the month, and that the terms of the supplier's statement are 2/10, net 30. This means there is a 2% discount off the total month's purchases if the statement is paid within 10 days of the month end, otherwise the statement is payable within 30 days without discount.

You thus have the use of the supplier's credit for 40 days if you take advantage of the discount; 60 days if you do not. In other words, you can use this "free" money to your advantage, even if all you do is collect bank interest on it.

On the other hand, suppose you purchase from the same supplier, but habitually buy at the end of each month sufficient goods to carry you through until the end of the next month. In this case you have the use of the "free" money for only 10 days if you take advantage of the discount, and for only 30 days if you don't.

These two cases are extreme, but they point out that wise purchasing can take advantage of a supplier's billing practices in order to increase your profits.

d. PURCHASE DISCOUNTS

Consider the benefits of taking a purchase discount whenever one is offered. For example, suppose the terms are 2/10, net 60. On a $5,000 purchase paid within 10 days you save $100 (2% of $5,000). This amounts to a considerable sum on all similar purchases during a year.

However, in the example given, you may have to borrow the money ($4,900) in order to make the payment within 10 days. Let us assume the money was borrowed for 50 days (60 days less 10 days) at a 10% interest rate. The interest expense on this borrowed money would be:

$$\frac{\$4,900 \times 50 \text{ days} \times 10\%}{365 \text{ days}} = \$67.12$$

In this case, it is advantageous to borrow the money since the discount saving of $100 is greater than the interest expense of $67.12.

17
INVENTORY

As a retailer, you need to have the right products for the right customer at the right time. Without that you have no sales. The objective in ordering the right quantity is to avoid running out of items (stockouts) while minimizing the investment or money tied up in inventory. Funds needlessly tied up in inventory are not earning a profit (in fact, carrying an inventory costs money). If you left money in the bank rather than putting it into inventory, it would be earning a profit — the interest rate paid you by the bank. In other words, the problem is one of both physical and financial control of your inventory.

a. PERPETUAL INVENTORY CARDS

In order to know how much to order of an item at any one time, you need to know how much of it you have in inventory. One good way of keeping track of the inventory you have on hand, particularly if you do not carry hundreds of different items, is to use a perpetual inventory card system.

An individual card is required for each type of item carried in inventory. A sample card is illustrated in Sample #14. The "In" column figures are taken from the invoices delivered with the goods. The figures in the "Out" column are for items sold.

1. Quantity control

Obviously, if all "In" and "Out" figures are properly recorded on the cards, the "Balance" figure on the card should agree with the actual count of the item on the shelf or rack. Thus, the cards can be useful in inventory control.

The cards also help ensure that items are not overstocked or understocked since they can show the maximum inventory for each item and the minimum stock level before the item needs to be reordered.

Without having to count quantities of items actually in stock, the person responsible only has to go through each of the cards once a week, or however frequently it is practical to reorder, list all items for which the "Balance" figure is at or close to the minimum point, and order the quantity required to bring the inventory up to par.

Note that the cards can also be designed to carry the names and telephone numbers of suggested suppliers.

2. Usage rate

To establish par, or maximum, stock and reorder levels, you must consider the usage rate of the item and the time lag between ordering and delivery (including possible delivery delays).

For example, suppose your shop normally sells 18 of one item a week (or 3 a day) and you order every 2 weeks. Normally, therefore, 36 would be ordered each time. However, a safety or minimum level of 6 for that item has been established. Therefore, par stock is 42, and minimum stock 6. If, on the order day, there are 9 in stock and 2 days are required for delivery, then 39 should be ordered since that is the amount that will bring the par stock up to 42 in 2 days when it will be needed.

3. Electronic registers

The perpetual inventory card system illustrated in Sample #14 is a handwritten one.

PERPETUAL INVENTORY CARD

PERPETUAL INVENTORY CARD

Item _____

Minimum _____

Maximum _____

Supplier _____ Tel. No. _____

Supplier _____ Tel. No. _____

Supplier _____ Tel. No. _____

Date	In	Out	Balance	Item Cost Information

90

Electronic equipment is now available that can accomplish the same purpose and provide additional useful inventory control information at very fast speeds.

For example, your inventory can be keyed into cash register sales so that each time a particular item is sold it is automatically deducted from the "perpetual" inventory of that item. The register is then programmed to provide you with an updated inventory of all items as frequently as you need it.

b. THE ABC METHOD

In operations that have hundreds of different items in inventory, you need not be as concerned about frequently ordering every item; concentrate on those items that constitute the highest dollar volume. One way to do this is to use the ABC method.

You must first prepare a list of all items in inventory and their annual usage quantities. Then multiply these quantities by the relevant cost prices to arrive at a dollar volume. These dollar volume figures are then classified as A, B, or C items according to their annual value.

Take a look at a partial inventory list at the bottom of this page and its ABC classification. Note that items 3 and 4 are considered class A items since the combination of the quantity used and their cost gives a large annual value. These items deserve the most attention since a change in either usage or cost can have a substantial effect on inventory. It might also be a good idea to order fewer of these items at a time since less money is then tied up in inventory at any one time.

At the other end of the scale are items 2 and 5 that, relatively speaking, constitute only a small part of total inventory value. They are class C items. Time and money spent on controlling these items may not be worth the effort and buying a year's supply of these items at a time would not have much effect on inventory.

The remaining items are in class B and it would be a matter of judgment as to the effort made in controlling those items.

c. SPECIAL PROBLEMS

Retail businesses sometimes have special inventory problems. Retailers may find their customers' demands change in the very short run with a change in market characteristics, clothing style changes (for a clothing store), or even with the weather (for example, an ice cream parlor).

Therefore, for retailers with special problems, the following might help.

(a) If circumstances permit, use perpetual inventory cards, or electronic registers for controlling inventory usage.

Item	Annual usage	Item cost	Annual value	Class
1	500	$ 2.00	$ 1,000	B
2	1,000	0.50	500	C
3	700	30.00	21,000	A
4	400	15.00	6,000	A
5	2,200	0.10	220	C
etc.				

(b) Alternatively, have a detachable portion of a sales tag attached to each item. This detachable portion can be taken off at the time of sale. Manually tabulating these tags can then tell you what is selling and what needs to be reordered.

(c) Establish a minimum reorder point and maximum inventory level for each basic item in stock. Your basic items are your big sellers that are more subject to market changes, and you want to ensure that you have the best possible quantity on hand at all times.

(d) If your business is quite small or carries only a few items, a form of visual control may be used, particularly if replacement items are readily available from suppliers. Visual control means that you can do away with inventory control paperwork. Items can be quickly counted in their respective storage locations and at each location there can be an indication (for example, pencilled onto a shelf or rack) of the reorder point. There are some risks of losing inventory control with this system compared to a perpetual inventory card system, but those risks are minimal if you stay on top of the situation.

In addition, you may find from your inventory control system that you have slow selling items in stock that you may eventually have to sell at less than normal markup and, in some cases, at less than cost. Retail stores selling items subject to style fads are particularly prone to this situation.

Good merchandising requires that you move those items out of your inventory as soon as possible. The cash tied up in such items is no use to you and you may only be able to move them with special sales, markdowns, and special advertising.

d. TAKING INVENTORY

Periodically, a complete physical inventory should be taken and its total value at either cost or selling price calculated.

This should be done at least once a year. In some cases, it is appropriate to take inventory twice or four times a year. In certain businesses, for control purposes, a monthly inventory should be taken.

For many retailers, with today's electronic sales registers, taking inventory is much less time consuming than previously since each time an item is sold and rung up, the inventory record in the register for that item is automatically reduced. In other words, the register can provide your inventory for you.

Frequent inventory taking provides you with a more complete safeguard against pilfering, theft, damage, slow moving merchandise, and similar inventory problems that cost you money.

One useful inventory control technique is inventory turnover. Calculating inventory turnover by total inventory, or even by major categories of inventory, shows you in a general way whether you have too little or too much money tied up in inventory.

Inventory turnover is calculated as follows:

Cost of goods sold
Average inventory

Cost of goods sold is Beginning of year inventory + Purchases for year - End of year inventory.
Average inventory is (Beginning inventory + Ending inventory) ÷ 2.
Using the following figures:

Beginning inventory	$55,000
Purchases for year	$490,000
Ending inventory	$45,000

the inventory turnover would be:

$$\frac{\$55,000 + \$290,000 - \$45,000}{(\$55,000 + \$45,000)/2} = \frac{\$300,000}{\$50,000} = 6 \text{ times}$$

Generally, the higher the turnover rate, the lower the amount of money invested in inventory, and vice versa. The inventory turnover rate can vary widely from one type of business to another, and even for businesses of the same type, although average figures for various types of business can be determined. For your business, try to find out the most appropriate level of turnover to avoid stockouts or carrying too much inventory, and watch for deviations from that level.

Where it is appropriate, you might also classify your merchandise into different categories and calculate inventory turnover by category. You will probably find that different categories (for example, shirts versus slacks in a men's clothing store) have quite different turnover ratios.

Also, in the above example, it is assumed that inventory is valued at cost price. In some businesses, it is preferable to value inventory on hand at selling price. In that case the equation would be:

$$\frac{\text{Sales for the period}}{\text{Average inventory at selling price}}$$

e. COST OF HOLDING INVENTORY

Some of the costs of holding inventory are:

(a) Financing — money borrowed to purchase inventory

(b) Storage — the space built or leased to accommodate the inventory

(c) Insurance — for loss of inventory in a fire or similar event

(d) Deterioration or obsolescence — some inventory items have a limited shelf life because of style changes (clothing store) or spoilage (in the case of perishable items in a restaurant)

(e) Breakage/damage

(f) Opportunity cost — when the money you use to purchase inventory could have been used to do something else. For example, if the money could have been left in the bank to collect interest

at 10%, the opportunity cost of that money is 10%.

These various costs of holding inventory can add up to as much as 20% to 30% of the total value of that inventory. In other words, for each $1,000 of inventory, the cost of holding it could range from $200 to $300 per year.

f. INVENTORY VALUATION

One problem that all businesses, small or large, face is periodic inventory valuation. This is usually done at each fiscal year end, and in some businesses at each month end. The inventory count is only accurate at the time it is taken and requires that inventory transactions be stopped at that time or that those transactions be adjusted for later.

A number of different methods of valuing inventory are available.

1. Lower of cost or market

A traditional method of valuing inventory is at lower of cost or market.

Assume you purchased 100 of a particular item on January 1 at $10 each, and 100 on June 1 at $11 each. At December 31 you have an inventory of 100 of that item on hand, 20 from the January 1 purchase, and 80 from the June 1 purchase. Cost value of that inventory is therefore:

20 x $10 =	$ 200
80 x $11 =	$ 880
Total	$1,080

If market price on December 31 for that item was $12, or 100 x $12 = $1,200, then inventory would be valued at $1,080, rather than $1,200 since that is the lower of cost or market.

In inflationary times, cost is generally lower than market price.

2. First in, first out

Another method of valuing inventory is first in, first out or FIFO. FIFO assumes that inventory is used up or sold in a business in the same sequence as it is purchased (the first items purchased are the first items used or sold) even though that may not always be the case in practice.

In the previous example, under FIFO the inventory value at December 31 would be:

100 x $11 = $1,100

In other words, it is assumed that the 100 you have on hand are all from the June 1 purchase.

3. Last in, first out

The last in, first out (LIFO) method assumes that the most recently purchased items are the first ones used or sold even though, again, this may not be the case in practice.

With the same example, the 100 items on hand on December 31 are assumed to be from the January 1 purchase:

100 x $10 = $1,000

4. Weighted average cost

With the weighted average cost method of valuing inventory, the value in our example is:

January 1	100 x $10 =	$1,000
June 1	100 x $11 =	$1,100
Totals	200	$2,100

The weighted average cost is:

$$\frac{\$2,100}{200} = \$10.50$$

The December 31 year end inventory value is therefore:

100 x $10.50 = $1,050

5. Comparison of methods

A comparison of the methods shows:

Lower of cost or market $1,080

FIFO 1,100

LIFO 1,000

Weighted average 1,050

As you can see, the value of our inventory, depending on the method used. It could be as low as $1,000 (LIFO) and as high as $1,100 (FIFO).

6. Special problems

Retail stores sometimes have a special problem with inventory valuation if they carry hundreds of different items. If computer assistance is not available, the time required to keep track of purchases and cost prices of each item still on hand at year end is horrendous.

To simplify the problem, those who count the items on hand at year end simply record the retail value (selling price) of the item on the inventory sheets. The average markup on retail price that is typical of the business can then be applied to that total retail value to arrive at inventory value.

For example, assume that total year end inventory value at retail prices is $100,000, and that normal markup on retail is 40%, then inventory value is 60% (100% - 40%) of retail or 60% x $100,000 = $60,000.

7. In summary

In general, choose the method of inventory valuation that makes the most sense from a business point of view. In addition, from an accounting point of view, the same method should be used consistently from year to year unless there is a valid reason to change it. Finally, the tax department also insists that the inventory value at the end of the year be the same as the inventory value used on the first day of the following year.

18
PRICING

Another important aspect of merchandising is product pricing. Before an item is sold from manufacturer to wholesaler, from wholesaler to retailer, and eventually from retailer to consumer, someone has to make a decision about the price to be charged. For some retailers this is easy since the manufacturer may provide a suggested retail price, although this does not prevent the retailer from selling at more or less than that price because of competition or other factors.

a. PERCEIVED VALUE

Generally, the eventual price of an item is what is conceived to be its value by its purchasers. Economists use the term "supply and demand" to describe this. In other words, the quantity or supply available of an item, when related to the demand for that item, dictates an appropriate price in the market.

For example, if you ran the only hardware store in town and a customer was desperate to buy a particular tool to finish a construction job, you could theoretically charge whatever you liked since supply is low (or at least controlled by you) and the demand is high. Of course, your asking price might reach a point where it would pay that customer to drive to the next town (where there are two hardware stores) and benefit from a lower price because of competition (i.e., increased supply).

This is a very simplified example, but it does show that, for every product and service, whether at the manufacturing, wholesaling, or retailing level, there is a relationship between supply, demand, and price.

Theoretically one could determine this exact relationship and price all goods and services accordingly, but it would be impractical and unnecessary to do this in real life since, even if only by trial and error, goods and service prices tend, over time, to stabilize at their "right" level if a marketing approach to pricing is used.

Under a marketing approach, you must consider what the customer is willing to pay, and what the customer is likely to expect for that price. In other words, does the customer feel that he or she is getting value for money at that price?

b. PRICING METHODS

1. Cost-plus method

In order to have a starting reference point in pricing, it is often useful to use a mathematical approach. The most easily used mathematical approach is that of cost-plus.

To use cost-plus, a specified percentage markup is applied to the cost of the item and then that amount is added to your cost to arrive at the selling price. For example, if an item costs you $40 and you apply a 50% markup to this cost price, your selling price will be $40 + (50% x $40) = $40 + $20 = $60. If this information were set up like an income (profit and loss) statement and you assumed other costs for operating and overhead were $12, there would be a profit of $8 on that item:

Sale	$60
Cost of sale	40
Markup	$20
Other costs	12
Profit	$ 8

In this particular case the markup covers all other operating and overhead costs and provides you with a satisfactory profit.

The difficulty is in arriving at a markup percent that does this because in many cases the other costs (operating and overhead) cannot readily be calculated for each item sold.

2. Traditional industry percent

In many businesses, a traditional industry percentage figure is applied. For example, retail clothing stores traditionally apply a 100% markup over cost since they know from experience that this level of markup provides them with a reasonable profit as long as the business is managed properly in all other aspects.

Other types of businesses use whatever the markup norm is for their type of business. The risk is that, for any particular business, because of some unique situation, this norm may not be appropriate.

For example, there may be damaged merchandise, shortages (from shoplifting or employee pilferage), employee discounts, and markdowns to move slow moving goods. The volume of these items may be difficult to determine, particularly for a new company, unless statistics from comparable companies can be obtained. Generally, they could range up to 5% of sales, therefore the markup that you establish must include a percentage of up to 5% of the sales value of those items.

Also, it is often not possible to use a standard markup on all items. In the past, some businesses were able to operate with a standard markup on every product handled. But today external factors necessitate that some items be marked up higher than the standard, and some lower, so that the overall average ends up being the desired figure. In other words, you must know your product mix and which items can be marked up more and which less.

3. Factors to consider

Some of the key factors to consider in establishing individual product prices include your marketing strategy, manufacturer's or wholesaler's suggested prices (where relevant), seasonal or cyclical nature of sales, nationally advertised prices, type of product(s) handled, policy on loss leaders (selling below cost where this can be done), competitor price policies, the market demand for various products, the desire to keep prices within a specified overall price range, and the need to cover costs to provide an adequate profit. Some of these items are discussed in more detail later in the chapter.

4. Confusion over markup

As stated, the markup is the difference between what it costs to purchase and process a product, including the profit desired, and its selling price.

The term markup is sometimes referred to as gross margin or gross profit, and it is frequently expressed as a percentage of the selling or retail price of the products instead of the cost price as illustrated above.

Because of this, you have to be very careful about using the term markup. Be sure that you or anyone else involved in calculating markups know whether you are using markup on cost or markup on retail or selling price. The two percentage figures are not the same.

For example, if we expressed the $20 markup (and remember it is 50% on cost) as a percentage of retail it would be:

$$\frac{\$20}{\$60} \quad \times \quad 100 \quad = 33\%$$

Why have both a markup on cost and a markup on retail that yield the same dollars of markup and give two quite different percentage figures? The reason is that it is generally initially easier to calculate markup on cost, but to better understand the costs of doing business it is probably easier to understand costs expressed as a percentage of sales or revenue.

On income statements, sales or revenue are usually given the figure of 100% and all other income statement figures are expressed in ratio to 100. For example, if we take our earlier income statement and put percentage figures alongside the dollars, the result would be:

Sale	$60	100%
Cost of sale	40	67
Markup	$20	33%
Other costs	12	20
Profit	$ 8	13%

The 50% markup on cost now shows as 33% on retail on the income statement. This can be useful information. For example, if you wished to increase profit on sales from 13% to 15%, one way to do this would be to increase the markup on sales from 33% to 35%. The question then is, what would this mean in terms of an increase in markup on cost?

Converting a markup on cost percent to a markup on retail percent is not difficult. Figures can be read from tables such as the one illustrated in Sample #15, or else a hand calculator can quickly do this for you using one or the other of the following two equations:

$$\text{\% markup on cost} = \frac{\text{\% markup on retail}}{100\% - \text{\% markup on retail}}$$

OR

$$\text{\% markup on retail} = \frac{\text{\% markup on cost}}{100\% + \text{\% markup on cost}}$$

In our case, we wish to change the markup on retail from 33% to 35%, therefore the markup on cost will change from 50% to:

$$\frac{35\%}{100\% - 35\%} = \frac{35\%}{65\%} = 54\%$$

and the new selling price of the item will be:

$$\$40 + (54\% \times \$40) = \$40 + \$21.60 = \$61.60$$

Can we be sure this is so? Let's calculate the markup on retail to be sure it is 35%:

$$\frac{\$21.60}{\$61.60} \times 100 = 35\%$$

5. Markdown

The opposite of a markup is a markdown. A markdown is a reduction of the retail price because of a sale or other reason. The markdown percent is invariably expressed as a percentage of the retail price and generally does not create the confusion that markups sometimes can. For example a 10% markdown of the $60 item discussed earlier would result in a price reduction of 10% x $60 or $6, making the new selling price $54.

Don't forget that when you mark down an item and anticipate selling more of that item to compensate, you should be aware of the additional sales required to make up for the markdown or price cut. Sample #16 shows some of these relationships.

For example, if your present markup on retail is 30%, and you cut your prices by 10%, you need to increase your sales by 50% to compensate! This is read by going to the 10% line in the left-hand column and reading the figure on the line under the column headed 30%.

From this table, it is evident that markdowns should not be used indiscriminately. In other words, establish a markdown that is acceptable to your profits without dealing them a death blow. Remember that your product mix and total sales must provide you with a gross profit

SAMPLE #15
MARKUP CONVERSION CHART

% MARKUP ON COST	% MARKUP ON RETAIL
10.00	9.09
11.11	10.00
20.00	16.67
25.00	20.00
30.00	23.08
33.33	25.00
40.00	28.57
42.86	30.00
50.00	33.33
60.00	37.50
66.67	40.00
70.00	41.18
75.00	42.86
80.00	44.44
90.00	47.37
100.00	50.00

SAMPLE #16
MARKDOWN CHART
(Showing percent of increased sales needed to maintain profit level)

	PRESENT MARKUP ON RETAIL							
PRICE CUT	5%	10%	15%	20%	25%	30%	35%	40%
1%	25.0%	11.1%	7.1%	5.3%	4.2%	3.4%	2.9%	2.6%
2	66.6	25.0	15.4	11.1	8.7	7.1	6.1	5.3
3	150.0	42.8	25.0	17.6	13.6	11.1	9.4	8.1
4	400.0	66.6	36.4	25.0	19.0	15.4	12.9	11.1
5	—	100.0	50.0	33.3	25.0	20.0	16.7	14.3
6	—	150.0	66.7	42.9	31.6	25.0	20.7	17.6
7	—	233.3	87.5	53.8	38.9	30.4	25.0	21.2
8	—	400.0	114.3	66.7	47.1	36.4	29.6	25.0
9	—	1000.0	150.0	81.8	56.3	42.9	34.6	29.0
10	—	—	200.0	100.0	66.7	50.0	40.0	33.3

that is adequate to cover remaining costs and provide a profit.

Markdowns should, therefore, only be used for slow or immovable inventory, to meet unanticipated competition, because your initial price was too high, because of seasonal changes or regular customer-anticipated sales, or for the introduction of new, lower priced products. In clothing and similar retail stores, style changes can also dictate the need for a markdown.

When deciding on a markdown percent, it is best to establish it at the maximum you are willing to take, for example, 20%. If you offer an initial 10%, followed by a later 10% this can disturb customers. The next time you offer a markdown sale the customer who might buy will wait in anticipation of a second markdown. If you don't intend to give one, that sale is lost.

A saying in the retail trade is that the first markdown is the best markdown. In other words, make the first markdown large enough to move the items so that inventory is reduced, cash is freed up, carrying charges are eliminated, and fresh, more profitable inventory can be purchased. Dead or slow moving inventory sitting on shelves or racks costs more and is worth less as time goes by.

6. Loss leaders

Markdown should be distinguished from loss leaders. Loss leaders are items sold at very appealing prices to generate customer traffic in the hope that these customers, as well as buying the loss leader, will also purchase additional items at regular prices or will return as regular customers in the future.

Loss leaders are normally well promoted and are offered for a short time. Loss leaders are not generally used for dead or slow moving inventory but rather for regular well-selling stock whose price you decide to reduce for a short period.

A secondary source for loss leaders is your manufacturer or wholesaler who sells you items at a lower than normal price so that you can in turn sell them as loss leaders. The manufacturer or wholesaler may pay for the promotional materials and/or advertising. The manufacturer or wholesaler does this to introduce a new product, or to stimulate the sales of a new item.

c. OTHER CONSIDERATIONS

As mentioned earlier, mathematical calculations give you a starting point in pricing. However, there are usually some other factors to consider.

1. Competition

With a marketing approach to pricing, you must also consider the competition. Regardless of your competition's location, you must keep its prices in mind. That does not mean your prices need to be identical.

For example, if you run a motel that is in competition with another one in the same block, your room rate might be a dollar or two higher than your competitor's (for an identical room) because you have a swimming pool while your competitor does not. Guests might be willing to pay the extra price for the swimming pool feature, even if they don't use it, simply because they perceive it as value for money.

2. Proximity to market

Proximity to market can also influence prices. If you run a retail store in a high volume shopping center convenient to its market (its customers) you might be able to charge more for identical products than in a similar shop in a less convenient (for its customers) shopping mall several miles away. However, the price differential cannot be too great; otherwise customers might well put up with the inconvenience of driving to the other mall to save money.

3. Alternative goods or services

Another variable in the pricing dilemma is the fact that all businesses, regardless of their nature, are in competition with each other. A potential customer of a travel agent can use the services of that travel agent for advice on vacation destinations, hotels, and even alternative ways of traveling there.

But that travel agent (and all the companies that it can act as an agent for) are also in competition with all other businesses that are not even in the travel business. The reason for this is that the customer does not have to spend limited resources (money) on a vacation. If the cost of a vacation appears to the customer to be too high, then the customer may just decide to spend the available money on new clothing, or a new car, or fixing up the house, or on any one of many other alternatives. Again, the customer's perception of value for money is the important factor. Prices must be fair to the customer otherwise you may not be long in business.

Remember also that the demand for your products is conditioned by factors such as supply availability, season, holidays, and trends.

4. Psychology

Psychology can also play a role in pricing. A $19.99 price tag seems to attract more people to buy than a tag of $20.00. Some retailers avoid ending their prices in even numbers or in 5s, particularly with low priced items. A 0.29 item is less than a 0.30 one, but it tends to sell more than if it were priced at 0.30 even if customers don't really care about the extra cent. They only think they do.

But don't forget that, for you, that reduction of 0.01 on a 0.30 item is equivalent to 1/30 or about 3% of gross profit, even though it may not mean that much to a customer. Alternatively, increasing a selling price from 0.41 to 0.43 means an increase of about 5% in your gross profit.

5. Economic factors

Economic factors are something that you can do little about in pricing but that you should nevertheless be aware of. Depressed economic conditions may force you to lower your prices, whereas a healthy economy may allow you to increase them.

If your retail business is in a company town suffering layoffs, your prices may have to be reduced. If company sales are expanding, your prices can be increased.

Finally, if you are in a tourist location, you may be able to increase your prices during the peak season, even though you have to lower them during the off season.

d. PENETRATION PRICING

Even though, over the long run, products tend to find their own right pricing, it is sometimes necessary to use special pricing techniques that are new to the market. If its price is initially too high, the product may never achieve sufficient sales for its seller to stay in business. If the price is too low, it may have the same result.

One method that is used to introduce a new product into a very competitive market is penetration pricing. The product is initiated into the market with a price low enough to cover costs, but little else.

Penetration pricing is often accompanied by heavy advertising, special sales, and frequent discounts. The objective is to convince the potential purchasers to buy the product once and then convert them to regular buyers. As repeat sales build up, and a healthy share of the market is achieved, the price is adjusted so that previous small profits (or even losses) are now compensated with respectable sales and profits.

e. SKIMMING THE MARKET

In some cases, with a brand new product, penetration pricing is not required. This is so when the product is so unique that, at least initially, there is no competition. In such cases, the manufacturer can establish

100

a high suggested retail price that customers are quite happy to pay since the demand is there. Eventually, new manufacturers may enter the market and force the price down, but, at least in the initial stages, the original manufacturer is able to skim the market.

A good example of this type of situation is hand-held calculators. When they first came on the market, they could handle only basic arithmetic calculations, but customers were prepared, even in those days, to pay $200 or more. Now the same calculator, with many more features added, might well sell for $20 or less. Although some of this reduced price is a result of improved technology, much of it is the result of more companies manufacturing calculators and more retailers selling them, causing increased competition.

f. PRICE LINES

Many products are sold in price lines. Price lining assumes that potential customers have an idea of the range of quality they want and the price they are willing to pay. Many manufacturers produce price lines with this in mind and produce three ranges of quality: good, better, and best. Sometimes there is a fourth range: budget.

Within each range of quality is a similar range of prices. Between each price range is a jump, or gap. For example, women's dresses may be stocked by a retail store in the $50 to $100 range, in the $125 to $175 range, and in the $200 and up range. If the customer wants a quality better than the $125 to $175 range, that customer has to pay $200 or more.

The philosophy behind price lining is that customers in their own minds establish price ranges for many of the products they buy. These price ranges identify the quality of the product the customer is willing to pay for.

Price lining can affect inventory since it means you will carry fewer items and larger quantities of each item. Those price lines that

generate the largest volume of sales are the ones that you stock in greater quantities.

g. SUMMARY OF PRICING STEPS

This chapter has shown some of the many possible approaches to pricing and some of the variables that need to be considered. In summary, a general approach to pricing individual products entails the following four steps.

1. Identify the product price characteristics

Each product or service has its own pricing characteristics, such as supply and demand, the market's perception of value, the competition, and so on. You should try to identify particular characteristics that lead you to more than just a guess as to the price to charge.

2. Select a fair range of prices

The identifying characteristics from step 1 should indicate a range (from low to high) of prices for a product.

If the variety of products carried is so wide as to make this job too time consuming, you might want to have a range of prices from low to high for similar groups of products. You then apply a markup approach to calculate what price provides you with an appropriate profit, and then see how that price fits into the general range. If you are dealing with a new product, you might consider the penetration or skimming alternatives.

3. Choose a final price

Once steps 1 and 2 have been carried out, you have the foundation for establishing final prices, once again keeping competition and the market's perception of value for money in mind.

4. Evaluate the pricing results

Since pricing is an ongoing problem, you must keep evaluating the results of your pricing policies. Since the costs of your purchases and other business expenses change from time to time, so must your prices to ensure that you continue to earn reasonable profits and a satisfactory return on your investment. In particular, check whether you have misjudged your final prices and as a result have inventory that is not moving. At that point, you must seriously consider markdowns.

The evaluation step in pricing is probably the most important of the four. By sensible evaluation you can improve your approach to pricing and increase your future profits.

19
CREDIT

Before opening your new retail store, you have to make some decisions and establish some policies about credit granting. Extending credit to customers is a marketing tool that most businesses use to encourage sales. Not offering credit (unless a customer is a known bad risk) generally decreases sales.

In fact, larger retailers extend credit not only to increase sales but also because they sometimes earn as much, if not more, from the interest of extending credit as they do from the sale of the goods that the consumer used credit to buy.

Extending credit requires a business to have a lot more cash resources since it can take anywhere from 30 days to 3 years to receive all payments for goods sold on credit. A rule of thumb is that it can take three to five times more cash (since you still have to pay your bills) to extend credit than it does to operate a business on a cash only basis.

Your difficulty as a small business operator is not in extending credit, but in turning that credit into cash as soon as possible. Money tied up in accounts receivable costs you cash since you could otherwise have that money in a bank account earning interest.

The extent of credit granted by a particular business depends on such factors as type of business, location, competition, tradition, income level of customers, and the specific credit granting policies of your business as well as its cash flow requirements. Credit accounts for about 60% of overall retail sales. However, some retail businesses do not offer any credit.

During periods of rapid business expansion and healthy economic conditions, credit is easy to grant. However, in downturns or recessions credit extension needs to be much more strictly controlled in order to reduce losses (bad debts) from collections on receivables.

a. EXTERNAL CREDIT

Credit can be either external or internal. Most external credit that your business is likely to be involved with is extended from national or international credit cards. Before accepting any of these credit cards, you must make necessary arrangements with the credit card issuer.

The most popular credit cards are Visa, MasterCard, American Express, Diners Club, and Carte Blanche. When sales are made with credit cards, you are assured of full collection of those sales (assuming the credit card has not been black listed and you have been so advised), less the credit card company charge.

Visa and MasterCard are known as bank credit cards, and sales slips made out using those cards can be deposited just like cash the next day in the bank. With non-bank credit cards, you might not collect the cash for two or three weeks, even if you send in the credit card sales slips promptly. Therefore, your sales employees should be encouraged to accept bank credit cards rather than the others if the customer offers a choice.

Sales commission paid by you to the credit card issuer can be as high as 6% of the sale. The actual charge varies according to the volume of sales. Most small retailers pay the higher rates, although you should realize that, since the various credit card companies are in competition, the rates may be negotiable to a degree.

b. INTERNAL CREDIT

Internal credit is the credit offered directly by the business. You handle it from granting the credit through to collecting accounts receivable and converting them into cash. The costs of internal credit are generally those for the additional employees, or employee hours, needed to handle the credit paperwork and procedures. Some types of internal credit are as follows.

1. Consumer credit

Consumer credit is credit extended to purchasers with the understanding that they pay the account within a certain time limit (for example, 30 days). Most retailers charge the customer for the privilege of paying their account beyond a specified date.

With consumer credit some companies allow open accounts. This simply means that any time a customer purchases something it can be charged to the account. These accounts are usually closed off monthly, and a statement summarizing the purchases for the month is sent to the customer within a few days of the month end. The purchaser is expected to pay within, at the most, 10 days of receiving that statement. No interest is normally charged on these open accounts.

Any small business granting open account credit must be careful to whom it makes this available.

2. Revolving, installment, and budget accounts

In addition to open accounts, a company may also allow revolving accounts, installment accounts, and budget accounts.

Revolving accounts generally have an upper limit that can be charged. Purchases within that limit are allowed without question. At the end of each month, the customer is required to pay a specific amount, sometimes expressed as a percentage of the total amount owing. Interest is charged on the unpaid monthly balance. Customers using revolving credit seldom, if ever, reduce their account to a zero balance.

Installment accounts are primarily used for credit sales of larger purchases. The purchaser is required to make a down payment of 20% to 25%, and the balance is paid off in equal monthly installments that may spread over one, two, or even three years (seldom longer). Interest or carrying charges are added to the principal amount due. Installment accounts are protected by the seller carrying a chattel mortgage or a conditional sales contract on the goods sold. In this way the goods may be repossessed if payments are not made on the account. The customer receives title to the goods when the final payment is made.

Budget accounts are similar to installment accounts, but for smaller amounts, and for relatively short periods (usually between three and six months). A down payment may or may not be required. The customer is required to make equal payments over the months of the agreement. In addition, there may or may not be a service or interest charge.

3. Credit requirements

Most jurisdictions now have legislation governing some aspects of credit granting. Basically the laws require that both the dollar costs and the effective annual interest rate must be made clear to the purchaser before the purchase is made on credit. If this full cost of credit is not given, the purchaser is only required to pay the amount disclosed.

In addition, the purchaser has the right to expect responsible conduct from any business involved in gathering, storing, assembling, or using credit and personal information, as well as the right to know what is being reported and to whom it is reported, and the right to correct false information.

4. Cost of internal credit

Where a small retailing firm is financially strong enough to carry its own credit accounts, it must measure its costs of doing that against the cost of extending credit through credit cards. Credit costs include:

(a) Bookkeeping costs to record customer purchases and payments

(b) Printing costs for sales slips, month end statements, and envelopes

(c) Postage costs (no small item these days)

(d) Interest lost on cash (that could otherwise be left in the bank to earn interest) tied up in accounts receivable

(e) Collection costs on delinquent payments and actual bad debt losses

If the total of these costs is less than the commission paid to the credit card company, then it pays to offer your customers open credit despite the fact that the national trend seems to be more and more toward credit card sales. In fact, one more recent trend is for retailers, where it is legal, to offer consumers a discount of up to 5% for paying cash.

c. CREDIT PROCEDURES

It is a well understood business axiom that extending credit increases sales and, therefore, profit. However, this is only true if the losses from unpaid accounts (bad debts) and the extra administrative costs of granting credit are less than the additional profit generated from credit sales.

Toward this end a small business, just like a large one, should establish procedures for granting credit and ensure they are adhered to. Basic procedures include the following.

(a) Have the person requesting retail credit complete an application for credit on a form designed for your company's needs. This form should include basic personal information about the applicant, such as name, address, telephone number, past employment record, present employment and time in position, salary, family status and dependents, present assets (home and bank accounts, for example), and any amounts owing to other companies.

(b) If you are a member of a local credit bureau or agency, check this application data with them to determine the applicant's credit record and limits of credit placed on the applicant by other retailers.

(c) Given the above information and your own assessment of the situation, determine the credit limit you feel is appropriate. You may feel it is unwise to extend credit because the applicant is a high risk.

Advise the applicant of your credit limit decision and other terms of credit (for example, the time allowed for payment, discounts for early payment, and if any down payment is required).

(d) New account credits should be observed closely during the first few months to ensure credit limits are being followed and payments made promptly. In due course, the customer may be advised, if all has gone well, that the credit limit and other terms are being extended.

(e) Send invoices promptly since this allows customers to check the amounts and encourages early payment. If you forget or delay mailing invoices, the customer may feel that delay in paying is also allowed. If invoices are followed up by a month end statements summarizing all invoices for that month, send these statements promptly. Your terms of payment should be printed clearly on all invoices and statements. If a second statement has to be sent, have it printed or rubber stamped with an obvious reminder such as "PAST DUE" in bold print.

(f) Follow up delinquent accounts diligently. A 30-day account not paid within 60 days should be followed up with a second reminder statement. After a further 10 days, a phone call is recommended, and then a registered letter and enclosed statement with a warning that the account will be turned over to a collection agency or lawyer if payment is not received within 10 days (90 days after the first statement). Although the small firm, through knowing its customers personally, can often collect on delinquent accounts, if payment has not been received within the 90-day period, it should then turn the account over to a collection agency, or to its lawyer for legal action.

(g) Charge interest where necessary on overdue accounts and possibly even repossess goods where this is practical and possible.

(h) Cut off repeat delinquents who you don't feel are good risks any more. Use common sense and tact in order not to lose good customers who have temporary cash flow problems that will be overcome.

1. Cost of interest

To dramatize the effect of overextending credit, consider the case of a company whose average sale is $102 and average costs to achieve each sale are $100. In other words, profit per sale is $2. If the costs to produce a sale are financed with money borrowed from the bank at 15%, the interest cost to borrow each $100 from the bank for 30 days is $1.23. Thus, extending credit

for 30 days reduces your profit from $2 to $0.77 ($2 less $1.23). If credit is extended for 60 days, the interest cost is $2.46, or $0.46 more than your "profit." If this were typical of your company, you wouldn't stay in business for long!

2. Credit files

Keep a credit file for each customer. For a small business this file can be as simple as a small card filed alphabetically by customer name. In other cases, a file folder for each customer may be needed.

This file should have in it the customer's original credit application and credit terms given at that time. As credit terms change, update the file.

You might also want to make a note in each file concerning the customer's payment record. Your regular accounting records should be established so that they provide you with immediate information about slow paying or delinquent customers, and it is a good idea to transfer this information to the credit files so that it is available for quick reference.

3. Bad debts

As a guideline, most businesses that are efficient at minimizing their bad debt losses keep them below 2% of total credit sales. Firms that are less efficient may find that their losses are as high as 5% of their credit sales. Such high bad debt losses can seriously eat into profits. The longer a credit sale is left outstanding (not collected), the greater the likelihood that it will become a bad debt.

4. Personal checks

Cashing checks for customers and companies is a form of credit extension. You should have a policy on whether to accept personal checks, and if the policy is to accept them then protective procedures should be developed to ensure that losses are minimized from problems such as checks returned from the bank marked

"Not Sufficient Funds" or "No Account." Here are some suggestions:

(a) Ask for one or two pieces of identification if the customer is not known to you. This identification (such as a driver's license) should include the photograph and signature of the person. Compare the photograph with the customer and the signature with that on the check.

(b) Record identification information (for example, driver's license number) on the back of the check.

(c) Look for erasures or changes on the check. Anything that has been changed (for example, a date or an amount) should be initialled by the customer.

(d) Look for a difference between the amount written out and the amount in numbers. For example, it is easy to write the amount as "forty-five" and the figures as $54."

(e) Do not accept predated or postdated checks.

(f) Do not accept checks made payable to a third party that the customer wishes to simply endorse over to you.

(g) Do not accept a two-party check. A two-party check is one signed by a person other than the customer.

(h) Once a check is accepted, endorse it immediately with the company's "for deposit only" stamp. This prevents forged endorsements if the check is lost or stolen before you deposit it in the bank.

Most banks now have machines available 24 hours a day to enable bank card holders to obtain cash, and for this reason you should try to encourage cash sales or, alternatively, the use of credit cards.

20
ADVERTISING

For most retail businesses, advertising is an absolute necessity. However, in comparison to a large company, the small business is at a disadvantage in some ways when it comes to advertising since, to be effective, the advertising budget of the small company has to be a relatively larger percentage of the sales dollar.

The typical large firm, because of the size of its advertising budget, can also use advertising agencies with their professional staffs. The small firm can generally not afford this service since commission costs can amount to 15% of the amount spent on advertising, to which must be added the cost of artwork and photography.

However, regardless of the size of your retail business, some advertising is necessary and usually worth the cost since, apart from the initial new business it brings in, it also has a cumulative effect as customer goodwill is built up and products gain an identity.

An existing business that is successful has an established demand for its products. This established demand needs to be supported by continued advertising.

However, increased business for an existing retailer, and new business for a new retailer, generally depend on creating demand, or advertising that attracts new and old customers to new products.

Advertising is often referred to as sales promotion or persuasive communication and is intended to —

(a) advise potential new customers of your business and the products it sells,

(b) remind present customers of the products or services you offer and their prices, and

(c) persuade the customer that he or she needs a particular product or service now and that it should be purchased from you.

a. PLANNING ADVERTISING

You should view your advertising as an investment rather than an expense. Successful advertising is planned, it doesn't just happen. It should be planned anywhere from six months to one year ahead and should answer two important questions.

1. Why are you advertising?

The reason for advertising should go beyond simply attracting customers. It should include what you will emphasize in your advertising. Is it your company name, location, and types of products? Or does it stress the fact that you are new in business and have something different to offer?

Alternatively, it might emphasize individual products or product lines that are new or different. In other words, your advertising should have a purpose.

2. When are you going to advertise?

This question is often answered once your advertising purpose has been determined. For example, if you are in retail clothing, you likely want to advertise a new line in conjunction with its arrival in your store.

Alternatively, your advertising may need to coincide with special events (for example, Mother's Day), or time of the year (summer) or as a tie-in with a manufacturer's national advertising of a brand name product.

On the other hand, if your advertising is more to advise customers and potential customers that you are in business, your advertising times can be more flexible and less tied to specific times or product availability.

b. ADVERTISING BUDGETS

Advertising budgets are generally established as a percentage of sales. Some argue that the percentage should increase when sales decline (since at that time the products need the advertising) and decline when sales increase. Regardless of policy, the objective of advertising is to maximize the benefits of advertising within budget limitations.

A typical advertising budget amount for a retailer is from 3% to 5% of annual sales. But even among retailers the percentage can vary. A new retailer probably has to spend more than the same type of retailer who has been in business for some time. Where competition among similar businesses is strong each of them may then have to spend more on advertising.

Of the advertising budget, about 80% will probably be for newspaper, magazine, radio, television, or similar types of advertising, and the other 20% for developing the advertising message.

The advertising budget is generally higher during peak sales periods. Advertising during low sales periods can be ineffective.

If you have enough working capital, you should double your advertising budget during your first year and spend the extra amount within a month or two prior to opening.

For example, if your sales goal is $150,000 a year, and your advertising budget 4% of that, or $6,000 a year, set aside an additional $6,000 of pre-opening working capital for advertising to provide your potential market with information and/or to take away business from your competition.

Also note that, if your advertising budget is $6,000 a year, that does not mean you must spend $500 every month. Your budget should be related to the proposed sales each month. For example, if July sales are budgeted for $20,000, your advertising budget for July is $20,000 x 4% = $800, and if budgeted sales for November are $8,000, your advertising budget for that month is $8,000 x 4% = $320.

Note also that the advertising budget for any particular sales month should not be spent during that month. To benefit from advertising, you must spend the money up to a month ahead. In other words, the advertising budget for July's sales should be spent in June, and so on.

In spending your advertising budget, even though there are many advertising vehicles available, you should not even think of using them all, even if you could afford to. Concentrate on one or two. More of one or two is better than less of five or six. Also, within any one medium the same principle applies. For example, it is better to run five advertisements in one newspaper than one advertisement in five newspapers.

Specific types of advertising media are discussed in the next chapter.

c. PREPARING YOUR ADVERTISING MESSAGE

Preparing your advertising message is important. As a retailer, manufacturers and wholesalers can often help in developing good advertisements, and the media themselves (such as radio or newspaper) can help you plan effective advertising campaigns.

As mentioned earlier, you may be able to afford a professional advertising agency, but their commission is usually at least 15% on top of the total cost charged by the newspaper, journal, radio, or other medium used. If you use a direct mail agency, you also pay a commission, sometimes 20% or more, or else a fixed fee.

You should take care in any claims you make about your business, its products, and its prices. Untrue statements, or exaggerated or misleading ones, can cause you legal problems from customers who complain to their local department that deals with consumer and corporate matters.

To be doubly sure, carefully proofread your advertisements before they are finally printed to weed out any errors. Be particularly careful of advertisements prepared by someone else on your behalf.

d. KNOW YOUR MARKET

Probably the most important aspect of advertising is to carefully analyze and know your market so that you can then use the most appropriate media. In other words, who are your customers? The better you know your market the more cost effective your advertising will be since it can be directed more specifically at those people.

Once an advertising strategy has been designed, it should be maintained continuously and consistently, although this does not mean that, where the need arises, some occasional special advertising cannot be added.

Repetitive advertising (a minimum of six times is recommended) is also necessary to be effective for most advertising media.

e. MEASURING RESULTS

Finally, try to determine how effective the advertising is by measuring its results. There are many ways to do this, depending on the type of advertising, but one of the simplest is to ask your customers how they came to know about your product. If sufficient numbers of them state that it is as a result of an advertising message, this may help you determine if your advertising is on the right track.

21
ADVERTISING MEDIA

Advertising, or sales promotion, can be categorized as either direct or indirect.

a. DIRECT SALES PROMOTION

Direct sales promotion is sending a commercial message to the public to inform both established and potential customers, with the objective of increasing sales.

There are various forms of advertising media that the retailer can use to send its advertising message to its customers. Whichever medium you eventually select you must be sure that it is —

(a) within your budget,

(b) compatible with your image and product,

(c) suitable for your market and geographic area of business, and

(d) able to effectively serve your geographic area.

1. Newspapers

Newspapers are a common and popular advertising vehicle for retailers. If your store only services part of a city, then the local community newspaper might be preferable to the large city newspaper and also costs less. Newspapers offer flexibility (in size of advertisements and the day(s) you wish to advertise) and graphics.

Make sure you are familiar with the market area served by the newspaper and obtain its circulation figures. Newspaper advertising rates are based on circulation — the higher the circulation, the higher the cost. The advertising cost divided by the newspaper's circulation gives you a cost per reader for purposes of comparison.

Newspaper space is sold in lines or inches and columns. For example, a 2-column, 25-line advertisement costs the equivalent of 50 lines.

Newspapers also generally offer special contract rates when you agree to purchase a specified minimum number of column inches over a year. This can significantly reduce your cost per column inch.

2. Radio

For the retailer, local radio stations can often be a useful form of advertising. Radios can reach a wide range of customers with a short lead time, although repetitive advertising is generally required for it to have any effect, and repetition does cost money.

Radio advertising is usually sold in 10-, 15-, 30-, or 60-second "spots." The half- and one-minute spots are the most popular. Costs vary depending on time of day, listening audience size, and the particular radio station. Advertising just before the news, and from 7 a.m. to 9 a.m. and 4 p.m. to 6 p.m., probably costs more than the same ad halfway through an hour of music between 10 a.m. and 11 a.m.

Find out what the cost per thousand listeners is. For example, if a spot announcement costs $30 and reaches 5,000 people, your cost per thousand listeners is $6. This way you can compare costs from station to station, and from one time period to the next on each station.

Also, as with newspaper advertising, your cost per thousand decreases if you contract to run a specified minimum number of advertisements.

However, if you use this medium, be sure you use a station that is popular with your type of customers and that the advertising is timed when they are most likely listening.

3. Television

Television advertising is very expensive and is not used very often by the independent retailer. It does have the advantage of a visual impact that radio does not have but, in addition to the TV station's cost of time, you have production costs, that, even for a 30-second ad, can run into the tens of thousands of dollars.

4. Magazines

Magazines can be expensive, but may more directly reach the type of customer who has an interest in your products.

However, if your business is localized (as it might be in many retail stores), the expense of advertising in this medium may not be worth the cost other than in local magazines, such as tourist visitor guides.

An advantage of magazine advertising is that, unlike radio, television, or newspapers, magazines are around for long periods of time and can be read by a succession of people. However, the small business should advertise in them only with caution. Note that they may need from two to four months lead time to run your advertisement.

5. Direct mail

Direct mail can be an effective form of advertising, particularly if it can be selective (for example, mailing the advertising flyer or brochure to customers you have previously served). It is relatively inexpensive and its effectiveness is easy to measure.

Direct mail includes the use of business cards, postcards, coupons, catalogues, letters, circulars, and price lists. The rate of return in direct mail campaigns usually averages about 2% or 3%. In other words, if you send out 10,000 circulars, you might expect 200 to 300 people to respond in some way.

Handbills, or general flyers, are a form of direct mail. These flyers are generally unaddressed sheets that are distributed to a specified geographical area — generally to households. Their purpose is usually to feature certain products or special sales. Flyers are particularly suited to the retailer with a local market since the cost of advertising this way is relatively less than with most other media.

Direct mail flyers, as opposed to general flyers, are addressed to specific households of people who have been, or are likely to be, customers. They can be more effective than general flyers since they are individually addressed and are therefore less likely to be immediately junked (or so the theory says!).

If you wish, you can employ the services, at a cost, of direct mail companies who supply you with names and addresses of potential customers to augment your own lists. For example, if you ran a sporting goods store, you might be interested in obtaining a list of names and addresses of potential customers who are sports enthusiasts.

6. Directories

Directories, and in particular telephone Yellow Pages advertising, can also be useful if you are in a business where the customers might initially want to reach you by telephone (for example, a repair shop).

Since telephone directories are usually published annually, their advertising messages generally have a relatively long life and, apart from any other advertising, are essential for most retailers.

7. Public transportation

Public transportation (buses, subways, taxis) are another popular way to advertise.

However, it is difficult to assess the benefits of this method of advertising.

8. Highway billboards

Billboards can be expensive but are still used by many small businesses (for example, restaurants or motels) where they can be strategically located to catch the eye of potential customers.

Billboard advertising is relatively expensive both for billboard rent and advertisement production costs.

9. Other methods

Other advertising media include samples or catalogues; and specialty advertising on giveaway items (matches, calendars, shopping bags) on which the name, address, logo, or similar information about the product or company is listed. This type of advertising establishes goodwill and identity for future purchases.

An important advertising medium for retail stores is a point of purchase display. Such a display is similar to having a salesperson in the store. These displays are useful for capturing impulse shoppers. Studies show that up to 80% of impulse shopping is the result of a display. These displays are particularly useful for introducing new products and for special promotions.

b. INDIRECT SALES PROMOTION

In addition to the direct methods of advertising already detailed, you also have the opportunity of using the following, less direct, forms of advertising.

1. Publicity

Publicity, or public relations, is advertising that you don't have to pay for other than in time. Publicity is both an internal and an external opportunity for increasing sales.

Internal publicity includes how you treat your customers while they are on your premises, and how you treat your employees, since both customers and employees can be goodwill ambassadors for your business.

External publicity means letting people know about the good things your company is doing by releasing "news" items or photographs to local newspapers, radio stations, and even television stations.

For example, if your business sponsors a sports team, or participates in a charitable event, the local news media might like to know about this. Words and pictures go a long way in creating community goodwill that is part of public relations, and this type of advertising can be carried out with little, if any, cost.

Public relations establishes the general view of your business in the eyes of the community. This is not something that can be purchased since it stems from an attitude in the public's mind that has been created by the way you run your business, the way you treat your employees, the way you handle your customers.

If your public relations are good, you develop goodwill in the community. Poor public relations lead to ill will which can affect your business negatively.

2. Special occasion sales

Special event sales are used for holiday seasons, the start of the new school year, the anniversary of the start of your business, special discounts that you offer, and similar events. You use your regular advertising channels to make them known to potential customers.

Regular special occasion sales are a good way to keep established business, but they also help attract and keep new business.

Beware of having too many discount sales since customers may end up being unable to distinguish your regular prices from those marked down, or may simply defer their purchases until your next sale. You must keep the relationship in balance, and if you reduce your prices too frequently, you may have a larger volume of items sold, but you might also reduce your total desired sales and profits.

When planning discount sales, you must not only decide which items to include, but also ensure that you have enough of those items in stock to warrant advertising a sale. Double check your costs and calculate how much discount or markdown you need to move the items.

When calculating markdowns, remember that you can either mark down all regular prices by a specific percentage (for example, everything in the store reduced by 20%) or have selected markdowns for individual items or groups of items. With selective markdowns, there is a risk that customers will only buy those with the highest percentage markdown since they perceive those to be the best bargains.

3. Manufacturers' aids

Retailers can sometimes benefit from help given by their manufacturers or head office to promote sales. For example, individual McDonald's restaurants benefit from national advertising carried out by the head office.

This advertising might also take the form of the manufacturer providing window or floor displays to promote the products. Sometimes the manufacturer might even contribute cash directly toward a local advertising campaign. This cash could be as much as 5% of your total annual purchases from the manufacturer. However, there may be strings attached for these cooperative advertising dollars such as how and where to run the ad.

4. Direct contact by sales employees

For retailers, direct contact by sales personnel is critical since advertising, by itself, is often not sufficient. Advertising might make customers aware of your products, but the actual selling must be carried through by competent sales personnel.

Training salespeople is a basic criterion. Salespeople must have a thorough knowledge of all your available products and their prices and be able to advise potential customers of products that fit the needs of the customers.

5. Consumer promotion

You should not overlook the potential in advertising by consumer promotion. Consumer promotion includes coupons, discounts, trading stamps, samples, demonstrations, contests, and similar techniques.

6. Product packaging

Any retailer that handles products that are packaged must be conscious of the way in which packaging and/or styling helps indirect sales promotion. Generally attractive packaging appeals more to customers than competitive products in less appealing packaging. Even a carry-away plastic bag in which a customer can put a product purchased from you can be a form of sales promotion.

7. Customer relations

Every retailer has customers and must develop good customer relations in order to have satisfied customers. This involves such matters as speed in processing orders, handling complaints, handling returned goods, providing an extra service where possible, and going out of your way in unexpected or emergency situations. Good customer relations build business through word-of-mouth advertising.

114

22

INSURANCE

Every business operates with risk every day. A risk is the possibility of damage, injury, or loss. Generally a small business is less able to absorb losses from risk, and for this reason it is more important that you understand the kind of risks that are common.

Once the risks are known, policies can be established to minimize them. Almost any type of risk can be insured against, but to insure against every possible risk is prohibitively costly for most small companies.

a. BUILDING AND CONTENTS FIRE INSURANCE

If you own your own building, the basic type of insurance coverage required is for loss to building(s) and personal property on a stipulated peril basis (such as fire, lightning, and earthquake).

Generally, building insurance covers all permanent fixtures (including such items as heating, cooling, air-conditioning, elevators, and similar engineering and/or mechanical equipment) as well as signs attached to the business.

Normally one insurance policy is sufficient if you both own and operate the business and contents (equipment, fixtures, and inventory). If the business is leased, the lessor and you (the lessee) should each insure his or her own property.

Fire insurance on building and contents is the most frequently purchased insurance. Cost varies considerably from one situation to another. Most fire insurance policies are written for three-year periods, with premiums frequently adjusted annually.

1. Optional coverage

Building and contents insurance can be further protected by various types of optional insurance (since a standard insurance policy does not normally include these items) including any or all of the following:

(a) Extended coverage covers the property against all direct loss or damage due to such things as explosions, windstorms, hail, riot, aircraft, vehicles, and smoke.

(b) Glass insurance protects against replacement of plate glass windows accidentally or maliciously broken.

(c) Vandalism and malicious mischief protects against losses caused by either of these possibilities.

(d) Sprinkler insurance covers against leakage, freezing, or breakage of sprinkler installations. If this type of insurance is taken out, both building and contents should be insured.

(e) Boiler and machinery insurance covers damage to the property caused by explosion of boilers and resulting damage to machinery. The insurance could also cover bodily injury to persons other than employees. A boiler and machinery policy will likely call for periodic inspection of the related boiler and machinery.

(f) Flood and earthquake are optional insurance coverages that should be considered in areas where flood, earthquake, or both are considered possibilities.

(g) Signs covers damage to exterior signs, such as a neon advertising sign, for damage from such things as wind or malicious rock throwing.

2. Co-insurance

Insurance companies know from experience that fire damage to buildings seldom results in complete loss of the building. You, as a business owner, knowing this, might want to insure a $100,000 building for only $50,000. If you do, and a fire partially destroyed the building causing $40,000 damage, you might expect to collect the full $40,000 loss. To protect themselves against this, insurance companies generally require co-insurance in their policies.

Co-insurance means that the owner of a building cannot partially insure it and still expect to collect the full amount of a partial loss. Co-insurance requires the building owner to share any losses with the insurance company.

The most common co-insurance is 80% of building value. In other words, if 80% insurance is required, and the building is insured at only 60% of its value, you will recover 60/80 of any losses incurred. If there is a $40,000 fire, you will recover only 60/80 x $40,000 or $30,000.

On the other hand, if there is a fire that causes a complete loss of the building and you have 80% co-insurance, the insurance company only pays up to 80% of the insured value of the building. This means you share the insurance loss with the insurance company.

The only way to have protection in the event of a complete loss is to insure 100%, even if the co-insurance requirement is only 80%. If a property is insured for more than 80% of its market value, the insurance company pays any losses in full up to the face value of the policy. It will never pay more than the face value of the policy.

The formula for computing insurance company liability with 80% co-insurance is as follows:

$$\frac{\text{Face value of policy}}{\text{80\% of property value}} \times \frac{\text{Amount of}}{\text{loss incurred}}$$

Co-insurance is particularly important to watch out for if the value of your insured property is increasing.

b. LIABILITY INSURANCE

Your business is liable to claims for alleged injuries to customers, employees, or others with whom you do business, either on or off your premises. The broadest possible insurance protection that you can buy is a comprehensive general liability policy that covers you against all claims for injuries that occur. This can be supplemented by optional endorsements to cover other specific possibilities.

Optional liability insurance might be required for a business that has a garage or parking lot for the convenience of customers. Two specific types of insurance are necessary: automobile garage liability protects against any liability for bodily injury and property damage caused by an accident in the garage or on the parking lot, and garage keeper's liability covers liability for fire or theft of stored or parked vehicles.

Liability insurance can include not only physical injury, but also damage to the property of others, and liability for defects in merchandise that your business has sold, or even such things as food poisoning lawsuits by customers against a restaurant.

c. VEHICLE INSURANCE

Vehicle collision insurance is basic insurance if your business owns cars and/or trucks. This insurance can be purchased with both a full coverage policy that pays all losses from collision damage in full, or from a deductible policy that carries a lower premium but requires you to be

116

responsible for the first $50 or $100 of damage from each accident. Collision insurance covers damage to your vehicle as a result of hitting another vehicle or object.

Comprehensive policies are available to cover fire and theft losses on automobiles. These policies protect against damage or loss from flood, fire, hail, windstorm, riot, robbery in the vehicle, theft of the vehicle, and glass breakage. Collision damage is not included in these policies.

You might also need liability insurance against claims for bodily injury (public liability) and/or property damage resulting from the operation of the business's vehicles. Public liability covers damage done to a person (for example, someone struck by one of your vehicles). Property damage covers damage done to the property of others by one of your vehicles.

d. MARINE INSURANCE

Marine insurance covers merchandise while in transit. The two basic types are ocean and marine. Ocean insurance covers transportation of merchandise and products on water while inland marine insurance covers both land and water transportation. Insurance can cover both damage (from water, rust, or spoilage) and theft.

e. CRIME INSURANCE

Your business may frequently have large sums of cash on hand subject to both employee theft and armed robbery.

To protect against such losses, some insurance companies offer blanket crime policies with complete coverage on a package basis. Although individual types of crime insurance policies are available, blanket insurance is usually cheaper, and since total coverage for the full amount of losses under such policies is prohibitively expensive, most crime insurance policies include a deductible amount. Some of the crime insurance types of policy follow.

1. Fidelity bonds

Fidelity bonds insure against losses due to theft or other misappropriations of cash or inventory or other business property by employees. Only established losses are reimbursed.

This policy can be written as a blanket bond to cover all employees or it can be a schedule bond to limit it to those specific positions and employees who handle, or who have access to, cash, inventory, or similar items. In some situations, it may be preferable to bond specific employees where there are few employees who can be individually named.

Fidelity bonds do not have time limits. They run until canceled by either party. Fidelity bonds carry a penalty or maximum amount to be paid in the event of a loss.

2. Money and securities

Money and securities insurance covers losses that occur away from the business's premises (for example, a robbery of daily receipts being transported to the bank).

3. Robbery

Robbery insurance covers loss of goods stolen where there is an assault or threat of an assault, such as in a holdup.

4. Burglary

Burglary insurance covers the loss of inventory, money, or equipment from a break-in of your premises. Generally there must be signs of a forced entry.

5. Theft and shoplifting

Theft and shoplifting insurance covers loss of inventory, money, or equipment where there is no break-in or burglary involved and items were presumably stolen by employees, customers, or others.

6. Surety bonds

A surety bond protects you from losses caused by the failure of others to produce on schedule. For example, if you are having a new building constructed, and the construction company does not complete the building on time resulting in losses to you, you may recover those insured losses from the insurance company.

f. BUSINESS INTERRUPTION INSURANCE

A standard fire insurance policy pays you only for losses directly due to fire. Other indirect losses, referred to as consequential losses, may be a greater risk to your business than the fire damage itself but can be protected against by business interruption insurance.

If you have business interruption insurance, the business is reimbursed for loss of earnings, and ongoing expenses that occur (such as interest expense on a mortgage or rent) until normal business resumes. In addition, payroll costs for key employees can be completely covered, or covered for a specific period of time. With business interruption insurance, co-insurance (discussed earlier) may be required.

g. OTHER INSURANCE

Other types of insurance are available for such things as excessive bad debt losses (credit insurance) and shoplifting, but the insurance cost for most retailers is not worth the benefits. Management control (such as control over credit policies to reduce bad debt losses) is a far better mechanism.

h. WORKERS' COMPENSATION INSURANCE

As a retailer you must provide your employees with a safe work place, and safe equipment and tools. Also, you are also likely to legally be required to have workers' compensation insurance. This insurance fund is administered by the jurisdiction in which you operate.

The fund collects premiums from individual businesses. These premiums are generally based on payroll (for example 3% or $3 of insurance per $100 of payroll) according to the particular type of business's accident rate experience.

Depending on the type of business, the rate can vary from as low as 0.1% to as high as 25% or 30% of your payroll dollar. The fund is used to pay employees injured on the job until they are able to return to work, and should not be confused with government unemployment insurance.

i. LIFE INSURANCE

If your key employees are sufficiently important to your business, you may buy insurance on their lives, payable to your business. There are four basic types of life insurance:

(a) Term life

(b) Straight life

(c) Limited pay life

(d) Endowment life

Each of these types of insurance has its own features and, in addition, there are variations and combinations to each of them. To determine what is best in individual circumstances, discuss your situation with an insurance company or broker.

j. KEY PERSON INSURANCE

Banks, and other lending agencies, often require key person insurance when you borrow money. For example, if you wish to borrow $50,000, the bank may require that you take out a $50,000 life insurance policy on one or more key employees of your business, with the bank as beneficiary. In the event of accidental death of the insured, the bank would receive the face value of that insurance policy and could pay off any bank loan that you had.

Another type of key person insurance is a cross purchase plan where partners/shareholders in a business agree to take out insurance on each other's lives.

This allows the surviving owners to buy out the share of a deceased owner.

For example, if A, B, and C each have an equal interest in a business valued at $300,000, each buys a $50,000 life insurance policy on the other two. If A dies, then B and C each receive $50,000 and the combined amount of $100,000 is enough to buy A's share of the business.

When an insurance policy (other than term life) has been in effect for a few years, it builds up a loan value. This loan value may be used to assist you in times of cash shortage since it can be assigned as collateral against loans. The full face value of the policy remains in effect during the period of the loan, subject to the amount of the outstanding loan.

23

ACCOUNTING RECORDS AND INTERNAL CONTROL

It is in your best interest to institute and maintain a complete record of all your business's financial transactions. The law requires that you keep certain accounting records for income tax purposes, and the better you keep these records, the easier it will be to complete your business's year end tax return and take advantage of tax savings possibilities like depreciation on fixtures, equipment, automotive vehicles, and your building if you own it.

Well documented accounting records support the accuracy of your tax return. If your records are incomplete and do not allow you, for example, to calculate your taxable profits, the tax department may have to use methods of calculation that are time consuming and may be disadvantageous to you since the tax you have to pay may be more than it would otherwise be if you kept proper records.

The actual books or records you keep depend on the size, nature, and scope of your business. The extent of the records also depends on the needs of your business and the extent to which you wish to be informed about it.

Unless you have a background in accounting you probably do not want to set up an accounting and control system by yourself; get your accountant to do this for you. However, if you do the daily routine recordkeeping yourself, leaving only the month end work for your accountant, the lower your accountant's cost to you is.

In addition you would probably be wise to have your accountant prepare your year end tax return since your accountant is up to date on the most recent tax regulations and can make use of all avenues to minimize the amount of tax your business has to pay.

a. BASIC ACCOUNTING INFORMATION

There is some basic information that any business needs to have a record of. First, sales (sometimes called revenue) by the day, week, month, or quarter; further broken down into cash or credit, by type of credit card if necessary; by department, type of merchandise, or kind of product should be recorded. Credit records are necessary in order to determine the amount of accounts receivable (money owed to you) at any particular time. Electronic registers can readily provide much of the required detail concerning sales without requiring extensive paperwork.

Operating expenses by type (for example, purchases, supplies, rent) in total by sales period, and even by department, or type of merchandise or product should also be recorded. In addition, you need to know the unpaid expenses that form your accounts payable.

The payroll is a major expense for most firms and one that has legal requirements as far as the detail that you must record is concerned. In particular, payroll withholding (e.g., unemployment insurance) must be properly documented.

Inventory should be taken at least annually and, in certain businesses, as frequently as monthly. Inventory must be separated by type, and even by item. Electronic sales registers can often be used to record reductions in inventory as a result of a sale. For more information on inventory, see chapter 17.

For all sales and expenses, it is important that you keep all documents supporting transactions: sales slips, register tapes, or invoices; purchase invoices and/or receiving reports; canceled checks for both operating expenses and payroll; and receipts or memos for cash payouts not otherwise supported by an invoice or check.

If you do wish to set up your own accounting records with minimal help from an outside accountant, you might want to read *Basic Accounting for the Small Business* and *Understanding and Managing Financial Information*, two other titles in the Self-Counsel Series.

b. CASH RECEIPTS

Your accounting system should be established so that it gives you good control over cash receipts.

Good cash handling and internal control procedures are not only important to the business owner or manager, but also to the employees involved since a good system shows that employees have handled their responsibilities correctly and honestly.

All cash receipts should be deposited intact each day in the bank. A deposit slip stamped by the bank should be kept by the business. This is your receipt. If all cash received is deposited daily, no one who handles it will be tempted to "borrow" cash for a few days for personal use.

It also ensures that no payments are made in cash on invoices. If this were allowed, a dishonest employee could make out a false invoice and collect cash for it.

Employees who handle cash (and other assets such as inventories) should be bonded. This way, losses are less likely to occur since the employee knows he or she has to answer to the insurance company if shortages arise.

1. Separate recordkeeping and asset control

One of the most important principles of good cash control is to separate the functions of recording information about cash and control of the cash.

Consider the accounts of the people to whom you sell goods or services on credit. These accounts are an asset. Suppose checks received in payment are given to the cashier who then records the payments on the accounts. These checks, along with other cash and checks received from customers, are turned in as part of the total remittance at the end of the cashier's shift. There is nothing wrong with this procedure as long as the cashier is honest.

2. Lapping

However, a dishonest cashier could practise a procedure known as lapping. Suppose A owes you $150 on account. When he receives his statement, he sends in a check for $150. The cashier does not record the payment on A's account. Instead the check is simply put in the cash drawer and $150 in bills is removed for personal use by the cashier. The cashier's remittance at the end of the shift balances, but A's account stills shows an unpaid amount of $150.

When B, who has an account for $170, sends in her payment, the cashier records $150 as a payment on A's account, puts the $170 check in the cash drawer and removes a further $20 in cash for personal use.

A few days later C's payment of $200 on his account is received. The cashier records $170 on B's account, puts the $200 check in the cash drawer and takes out $30 more in cash.

This lapping of accounts eventually increases to the point where the cashier can no longer cover a particular account and the fraud is discovered. However, the outstanding account may be so large that the misappropriated cash cannot be recovered from the dishonest cashier.

To help prevent this type of loss, institute separate cash receiving and recording on accounts. Checks or cash received in the mail in payment of accounts should be deposited directly in the bank by you or a responsible employee.

The employee looking after the accounts is simply given a list of account names and amounts received, and the appropriate accounts can be credited without the person handling any money. In other words, the responsibility for handling cash and for recording payments on accounts are separate.

c. CASH DISBURSEMENTS

For minor disbursements that have to be handled by cash, a petty cash fund should be established. You should put enough cash into this fund to take care of about one month's transactions. The fund should be the responsibility of one person only. Payments out of it must be supported by a receipt, voucher, or memorandum explaining the purpose of the disbursement.

When the cash fund is almost used up, the supporting receipts, vouchers, and memoranda can be turned in and on the head cashier's or manager's authority, the fund is replenished with cash up to the original amount. Receipts, vouchers, or memoranda turned in should be stamped "paid," or canceled in some similar way, so that they cannot be reused.

All other disbursements should be made by check and supported by an approved invoice. All checks should be numbered in sequence. Checks should be prepared by you or a responsible person, but that other person should have no authority to sign the checks.

As checks are prepared, the related invoices should be canceled in some way so that there is no possibility of their being fraudulently reused. Any checks spoiled in preparation should be voided in some way so that they cannot be reused.

d. BANK RECONCILIATION

One control that is necessary in a good internal control system is a monthly bank reconciliation. At each month end you should obtain a statement from your bank showing each daily deposit, the amount of each check paid, and other items added to or subtracted from the bank balance. The canceled (paid) checks should accompany this statement.

The steps in the reconciliation are:

(a) Compare and mark off on the statement the amount of each check received with your bank statement.

(b) Arrange your canceled (paid) checks in numbered sequence.

(c) Verify the amount of each canceled check with the amount on your check register or journal. Make a note of any outstanding checks. An outstanding check is one made out by you but not yet paid by the bank.

(d) To the bank statement balance add deposits made by you and not yet recorded by the bank and subtract any outstanding checks.

(e) To your bank balance add any amounts added by the bank on its statement but not yet recorded by you (for example, bank interest earned on deposits) and subtract any deductions made by the bank (such as automatic payments on loans, and interest or service charges).

Once steps (a) to (e) have been completed, the two balances should agree. If they do not, the work should be checked. If the figures still do not agree, then errors have been made, either by the bank or on your books. These errors should be discovered and corrected.

To illustrate how a reconciliation is carried out, consider the following hypothetical figures:

Bank statement balance	$4,456
Company bank balance	6,848
Deposit in transit	2,896
Outstanding checks	
— #355	372
— #372	40
Interest earned on deposits	98
Bank service charge	6

The reconciliation would be as follows:

Bank balance	Your balance
$4,456	$6,848
2,896	98
(372)	(6)
(40)	
$6,940	$6,940

To ensure control, the bank reconciliation should not be carried out by the person who records cash receipts or disbursements, otherwise "kiting" could occur. Kiting occurs when a check is written or drawn on bank account A without recording it as a disbursement. The check is then deposited in bank account B and the deposit is recorded. As a result, the cash amount in bank A is overstated (and cash can be removed) by an amount equal to the unrecorded check.

If you have enjoyed this book and would like to receive a free catalogue of all Self-counsel titles, please write to

Self-Counsel Press
1704 N. State Street
Bellingham, Washington   98225